Getting Started with CouchDB

MC Brown

Beijing · Cambridge · Farnham · Köln · Sebastopol · Tokyo

Getting Started with CouchDB

by MC Brown

Published by O'Reilly Media, Inc., 1005 Gravenstein Highway North, Sebastopol, CA 95472.

O'Reilly books may be purchased for educational, business, or sales promotional use. Online editions are also available for most titles (*http://my.safaribooksonline.com*). For more information, contact our corporate/institutional sales department: (800) 998-9938 or *corporate@oreilly.com*.

Editor: Julie Steele	**Cover Designer:** Karen Montgomery
Production Editor: Melanie Yarbrough	**Interior Designer:** David Futato
	Illustrator: Robert Romano

Revision History for the First Edition:
    2012-01-25   First release
See *http://oreilly.com/catalog/errata.csp?isbn=9781449307554* for release details.

ISBN: 978-1-449-30755-4

[LSI]

1327502920

Table of Contents

Preface

Introduction

When I was about nine years old, I had an Acorn Electron, a home computer developed by Acorn Machines and one of the major precursors to modern home computing. It was tiny by today's standards, having just 32K of RAM, a 2MHz CPU, and with the staggering ability to store a massive 360 Kb on the 3 inch Amstrad disks I was using at the time. It wasn't my first machine; I cut my teeth on the Sinclair ZX81 and later the ZX Spectrum. Despite all these limitations, I built numerous different pieces of software for myself, including my very first database for my second greatest passion, books.

Through the yeras, I've worked on many different database systems, including dB III+, Microsoft Access, Oracle, BRS, Filemaker, Omni 4D, and what I'm probably best known for, MySQL. The fundamentals of wanting to store information and retrieve it very quickly are all possible using these tools and just as I did in 1983, I've built some fun and serious applications in all of them. For the most part, though, the database became a tool—just another utility that became part of the toolkit for building the application.

Then I was introduced to Apache CouchDB, and I rediscovered the passion I had when developing applications on the Electron. Building databases was fun. They could be built quickly, without having to worry about drivers, languages, or indeed many of the complexities of querying and retrieving information. Most importantly, for any database application, I didn't have to worry about structures or how to get the information in a structured format.

When you read this book, that's the passion I hope you get—the realization that storing and retrieving information can be fun again with the help of CouchDB.

Conventions Used in This Book

The following typographical conventions are used in this book:

Italic
> Indicates new terms, URLs, email addresses, filenames, and file extensions.

Constant width

Used for program listings, as well as within paragraphs to refer to program elements such as variable or function names, databases, data types, environment variables, statements, and keywords.

Constant width bold

Shows commands or other text that should be typed literally by the user.

Constant width italic

Shows text that should be replaced with user-supplied values or by values determined by context.

> This icon signifies a tip, suggestion, or general note.

> This icon indicates a warning or caution.

Using Code Examples

This book is here to help you get your job done. In general, you may use the code in this book in your programs and documentation. You do not need to contact us for permission unless you're reproducing a significant portion of the code. For example, writing a program that uses several chunks of code from this book does not require permission. Selling or distributing a CD-ROM of examples from O'Reilly books does require permission. Answering a question by citing this book and quoting example code does not require permission. Incorporating a significant amount of example code from this book into your product's documentation does require permission.

We appreciate, but do not require, attribution. An attribution usually includes the title, author, publisher, and ISBN. For example: "*Getting Started with CouchDB* by MC Brown (O'Reilly). Copyright 2012 MC Brown, 978-1-449-30755-4."

If you feel your use of code examples falls outside fair use or the permission given above, feel free to contact us at *permissions@oreilly.com*.

Safari® Books Online

Safari Books Online is an on-demand digital library that lets you easily search over 7,500 technology and creative reference books and videos to find the answers you need quickly.

With a subscription, you can read any page and watch any video from our library online. Read books on your cell phone and mobile devices. Access new titles before they are available for print, and get exclusive access to manuscripts in development and post feedback for the authors. Copy and paste code samples, organize your favorites, download chapters, bookmark key sections, create notes, print out pages, and benefit from tons of other time-saving features.

O'Reilly Media has uploaded this book to the Safari Books Online service. To have full digital access to this book and others on similar topics from O'Reilly and other publishers, sign up for free at *http://my.safaribooksonline.com*.

How to Contact Us

Please address comments and questions concerning this book to the publisher:

O'Reilly Media, Inc.
1005 Gravenstein Highway North
Sebastopol, CA 95472
800-998-9938 (in the United States or Canada)
707-829-0515 (international or local)
707-829-0104 (fax)

We have a web page for this book, where we list errata, examples, and any additional information. You can access this page at:

http://shop.oreilly.com/product/0636920020837.do

To comment or ask technical questions about this book, send email to:

bookquestions@oreilly.com

For more information about our books, courses, conferences, and news, see our website at *http://www.oreilly.com*.

Find us on Facebook: *http://facebook.com/oreilly*

Follow us on Twitter: *http://twitter.com/oreillymedia*

Watch us on YouTube: *http://www.youtube.com/oreillymedia*

Acknowledgements

It should go without saying that without the brainchild of Damien Katz, this book wouldn't exist, and CouchDB in its current form wouldn't exist without the help and input of other CouchDB developers like Jan Lenhardt, J. Chris Anderson, Benjamin Young, and the other developers and team at CouchOne (now Couchbase). Thanks, as well, to James Phillips and Bob Wiederhold at Couchbase for supporting me while I developed this book. Bradley Holt has been a champion for CouchDB books for some time, and he provided help and support on this title. Finally, the ever patient folks at

O'Reilly, including, but not limited to, Mike Loukides, Julie Steele, and Melanie Yarbrough, who gave me the opportunity and helped me turn the raw text into a good looking book.

CHAPTER 1

Why CouchDB?

Traditional database systems have existed for many years, and they have a familiar structure and expected methods of communicating, inserting, and extracting information. Although complex to condense into a simple statement, most database systems rely on the creation of a specific structure (based on specific fields of information), organized collectively into a record of data. To get information in, you add a record of data, and to get the information out, you query the records by looking for values or ranges within those specific fields.

Apache CouchDB is different and one of a new breed of databases that relies on a different approach to the database structure, methods of storing information, and methods for retrieving it. There are many reasons why this new breed of database systems is required and for much of the motivation behind the development of CouchDB.

In this chapter, we're going to look at the basics of CouchDB, why it is different, and why the new approach has everybody excited about using CouchDB. CouchDB was produced out of the needs and necessities of the environment. Developers are becoming more savvy every year, with better environments, better tools, and simpler and more straightforward methods for achieving a range of goals.

You only have to look at the Web and the different tools and environments available. It is easy to take the effects of the modern websites for granted, but the functionality of pop-up lists during searches, customization, and the in-page experience (traditionally referred to as AJAX) of a dynamic website. Five years ago, this functionality was rare. Today, toolkits like jQuery or Dojo make this process easier. Outside of the Web, environments like Apple's Xcode or Microsoft's .NET all provide toolkits that simplify the development and functionality of your applications.

So how does CouchDB make these processes easier? Here are the highlights, some of which we will expand on in this and later chapters:

- An HTTP-based REST API makes communicating with the database easier, because so many modern environments are capable of talking HTTP. The simple structure of HTTP resources and methods (GET, PUT, DELETE) are easy to understand and develop with.

- The flexible document-based structure eliminates the need to worry about the structure of your data, either before or during your application development.
- Powerful mapping of your data to allow querying, combining, and filtering the information.
- Easy-to-use replication so that you can copy, share, and synchronize your data between databases, machines, and even continents.

Let's look at these features in more detail.

Learning to Relax

Perhaps most importantly, we will look at why the mantra when using CouchDB is *relax*, and why this message is printed out when you start the CouchDB database. CouchDB was built with web developers in mind, and anybody that was worked on the Web should be familiar with how it works. But CouchDB is also easy to understand even for non-web developers.

Relaxing with CouchDB falls into three main areas:

Interface
> Allowing database developers to develop their solutions without getting in the way with complex processes and interfaces was a key part of the design goal for CouchDB. Requiring drivers, interfaces, and complex protocols is counter to that process. CouchDB is therefore accessible through a simple HTTP-based REST API, and that makes it very simple and easy to use. We'll look at the basic mechanics of this interface later in this book.

Deployment
> Lots of databases work well during development, but the experience is not always shared during deployment. CouchDB tries to address some of the pain by allowing the deployment of a database or application to be simple and straightforward. CouchDB is fault-tolerant and generally self-sufficient. If something goes wrong, the problems are dealt with simply and gracefully; you can always obtain more detailed information if you need it. In general, if something goes wrong, it should be simple to find out what happened, but such issues are rare.

Scaling
> Scaling your database is another important element of the deployment process. Dealing with a range of different loads on the database can be difficult to handle. CouchDB will handle a temporary increase in concurrent requests without complaining. Each request may take longer, but it will still be handled.

> Furthermore, the issue of extending or expanding your deployed environment to support more requests is made easier through the simple structure of CouchDB.

Instead of enforcing the way you scale, CouchDB can easily be integrated with a variety of other solutions giving you the flexibility to use whichever system suits your needs best.

As a rule, the simplicity of CouchDB enables you to develop and deploy an application in a way that is both flexible and efficient. It is unlikely that CouchDB will let you get yourself into any difficulty without giving you some indication of where the problem lies.

A Different Data Model

I've touched on this already, but one of the key differences between CouchDB and other database solutions is the flexible nature of the format for storing information. Probably the best way to think about this is to look at an example.

If you look at a typical contact entry, it might look something like this:

```
Name: AN Other
Phone: 01234 567890
Email: an@example.org
```

When modeling this in a typical database you might create a field for the name, phone, and email. But problems can occur when you get another record that is outside of your structure:

```
Name: MC Brown
Phone: 01234 567890
Mobile: +44 1234 098765
Email: mc@example.org
Email: mc@couchbase.com
```

Here I have two email addresses and both phone and mobile numbers. Companies can introduce similar issues:

```
Name: Example
Phone: 01234 567890
Fax: 01234 098765
Email: info@example.org
Website: example.org
```

These are all fairly simple records for contacts. We haven't even considered complexities like postal addresses (or the fact that there might be more than one), and my contact record doesn't include additional details like my Skype IDs, instant messaging accounts, or that I have a few more addresses than those listed above.

If you think about how the contact information is used, for example on a business card, you can see that the data itself is important, even though the structure and method for storing information may not be. This is an example of where the semantics of the data (i.e., the type of information that is stored) is similar but the syntax and structure of the information varies significantly.

In a traditional database, there are many different ways of modeling this information, but a common one is to use relations to model the information. There is a core contact table, another table for each phone number, another for emails and IM, etc., and all this is then linked together using a unique ID so that you can obtain all the information you need.

There is nothing inherently wrong with this approach. In fact, in many cases there are some significant advantages to this approach when working with some types of data. However, the point here is that your data may not fit an arbitrary (and fixed) data model such as the one described here. It can even be difficult as the data matures and expands to know where the right place for information is. Twenty years ago, requirements like email, website, or Skype addresses won't have occurred to most designers.

Within CouchDB, the opposite approach is used. Rather than trying to create a structure into which all the information that you want to store can be shoehorned, CouchDB stores the data as documents, and worries about how to report and aggregate the information that is stored. Using our contact example, the information could be recorded in the database exactly as written it above, with each person's contact details stored as a CouchDB document. We can make the decision during the reporting phase on how to output information, what information to output, and indeed whether to output that data at all.

Replication

Databases are no longer isolated, single systems. Whether you want a database that can be shared among multiple devices (your desktop, laptop, and mobile phone), between multiple offices, or to be used as part of your database scaling operations, copying and sharing database information has become required functionality.

Different databases have traditionally approached this in a variety of different ways, including binary logs, data streams, row-based logging, and more complex hashing techniques. Within CouchDB, a simple but very effective method has been developed that uses the individual documents as the key to the method of sharing and distributing the document information between databases.

Note that the distinction is that replication occurs between databases, not necessarily instances of CouchDB. You can use replication to copy documents between databases on the same machine, the same database on different machines, and different databases across multiple machines and devices.

The simplicity and ease with which you can share and exchange information in this way is a key feature of CouchDB. The replication system uses the same REST API as the client interface to the database, and it supports the ability to filter and select records during the replication process.

Another useful aspect of CouchDB replication is that it operates one way. That is, if you have a desktop machine and a laptop and you want to replicate your data so that you can take it with you, you can perform a specific desktop to laptop replication. If you make changes to the database while you are away, replicate the changes back from the mobile to the desktop. Better still, you can replicate both ways and keep the two databases in sync. This approach simplifies the entire replication process and ensures that you can always replicate the data where you need it.

CouchDB allows you to create both the one-shot replication, and to configure replication that will continuously replicate changes to your configured database. In CouchDB 1.1 and later, the replication configuration is retained when restarting CouchDB.

The one-way nature of replication also means that you can replicate documents from multiple databases into a single database. For example, data collection or logging systems can use multiple CouchDB instances to collect information, then replicate the data all to one machine for processing and statistics.

CouchDB also handles problems with replication with ease. The Fallacies of Distributed Computing imply that all of the following are solved in a perfect system:

1. The network is reliable.
2. Latency is zero.
3. Bandwidth is infinite.
4. The network is secure.
5. Topology doesn't change.
6. There is one administrator.
7. Transport cost is zero.
8. The network is homogeneous.

The reality, of course, is quite different. Rather than expecting everything to work fine, CouchDB expects there to be a problem and tries to cope with it. Rather than treating a fault with replication as a serious problem, CouchDB instead tries to recover gracefully from the problem and only tells the user when there is a problem that requires user interaction. The replication process is also incremental, so that if anything goes wrong, such as a network outage, replication will pick right back up where it stopped.

One other ability is that replication information can also be filtered. For example, if you wanted to replicate only the contact information from one database into another, you can apply a filter to the replication process and copy only the documents that are marked as contacts. Or only replication records created in the last three months, or only those with an "r" in the month. The filter uses the same JavaScript as the other systems in CouchDB and is therefore immensely customizable to your needs.

To summarize, replication offers a number of potential scenarios:

- Replicate from database A to database B once

- Replicate from database A to database B continuously
- Replicate from database A to database B and B to A continuously
- Replicate from database A to B to C to D to E to A
- Replicate between databases A, B, C, D, and E
- Replicate from database A, B, C, and D to database E

You may think that all of this replication introduces some interesting issues when the same record is edited or modified on multiple machines. CouchDB has a solution for this, too, called conflict resolution. But to keep things simple, even the default response in the event of a conflict is consistent so that it doesn't stop your database from operating within a cluster.

Eventual Consistency

As you have seen in the previous section discussion on replication, the issue of distributing your data around different CouchDB instances is one way to take advantage of the functionality and flexibility that CouchDB offers.

One of the issues in a distributed system is the expectation that your network and system operate effectively and reliably. In a typical relational database management system (RDBMS) solution, for example, reliability and consistency, in particular, in a distributed system can start to be a problem. You rely on global state, timing, forced delays, and synchronous operations to ensure that your writes are available across your entire system before your application needs to read it back.

Within the three distinct concerns of *consistency*, *availability*, and *partition tolerance* of Brewer's CAP theorem on distributed applications, the RDBMS is relying on the C and A portions to support the distributed model. Different solutions approach the problem differently, but a common approach includes using a single database for writes and multiple for reads, which introduces the problem of synchronizing operations so that all clients get the right data.

That is, once you scale up your system beyond a single node and you start to distribute your load across multiple machines, you have to start worrying about how to make the data available, keep it consistent, and partition the information across the database to help support the distributed model.

CouchDB approaches the problem differently using what is called eventual consistency. If the availability of your database is a priority, then CouchDB can be used in a way that allows a single node to provide read and write support, and therefore consistency for the immediate user. The other nodes in the distributed system can catch up later, becoming eventually consistent with the other nodes as the data is updated. This can be achieved while providing high-availability of the data in question.

CouchDB employs other tricks to help improve this consistency model on a single node basis, and to improve the overall performance and throughput. There is no need to go into detail, but some of the features CouchDB uses include:

Key/value nature of the data store
> Key/value nature of the data store enables very quick access to the documents stored. Using a key to read or write a single document provides a huge advantage in terms of reading and writing over a row or lookup method.

B-tree storage engine for all internal data, documents, and views
> B-tree engines are quick for retrieving single keys and key ranges. Better still, the view model also allows for key/value data to be written directly into the B-tree storage engine automatically sorted by the key. This further improves single and range-based key lookups.

Lock-free database updates
> Traditional databases will lock an entire data store (table) or record while data is inserted or updated. CouchDB uses a Multi-Version Concurrency Control (MVCC) model. Instead of locking the database, CouchDB writes a new version of the existing record. This allows different processes to access old versions while the new version is being inserted, and also means that updating the information is really just a case of appending the new data, not reading, updating, and writing back a new version.

Freeform document format
> Most databases will enforce strict requirements on the format of the data and check and invalidate insert and update requests if they are not in the correct format. In many cases, your application can use the JSON object structure directly without having to serialize your objects or data into the fixed format required by the database engine.
>
> CouchDB can write the JSON document directly, simplifying the writing/update process, while allowing you to optionally enfore a structure on your JSON documents within the database itself if you need it. The enforcement and validation, though, continues to work with the JSON structure of the data.

By using these features, and the eventual consistency model within a distributed deployment, you can work with CouchDB to help support and improve your performance and latency, and to scale in a more linear fashion.

Data: Local, Remote, Everywhere

The CouchDB document-based approach solves another of the major issues in the modern world, which is one of access and ability. Although it is obvious we are moving to a fully connected world and environment, the reality is that there will always be a location, device, or situation where network access is unavailable.

Being in a lift, the middle of a desert, an airplane, or even just a simple powercut can all completely remove you from access to your database if it is only accessible in a single server or a cluster of servers in the cloud.

By allowing you to easily copy information from one database to another, CouchDB simplifies the problem of having the data where you need it. Instead of relying on one massive database you can access over the Internet, you can have a copy of the data you need on your laptop, iOS, or Android mobile phone, and then synchronize the information back to your big database.

The locality of the information also helps solve another problem commonly seen with network-based applications: the latency of access to the information. By storing the data locally and synchronizing the information in the background, the UI and response times can be kept high without losing the holistic approach to data storage.

This doesn't stop you from deploying CouchDB in the cloud or providing central services. Instead it provides you with flexibility for how and where you deploy and distribute your data.

CouchDB Deployment and Peformance

Looking over all the different features and functionality in this section, it should be clear that CouchDB can be used and employed in a variety of different ways.

One of the key issues for any modern database system is the problem of scaling and improving the performance of your database to cope with different loads. As a general rule, improving the performance in one area of your system typically has an effect on another area.

For example, increasing your throughput when you read or write information to and from your database will usually increase your latency of response. You can look at a variety of solutions at different points to improve that, but often the effects in one area alter the peformance and capabilities in another.

CouchDB doesn't attempt to solve your scalability problems with any single solution, but instead provides you with a simple and flexible system that can be molded and adapted to your needs. It is not going to solve every problem, and it's not designed to, but as a basic building block into a larger system, you can use the flexibility of replication to provide scale (both reading and writing), combine it with proxy services to improve latency during scaling, or combine different systems and combinations to provide a key points in different parts of your solution.

CHAPTER 2

Installation

For you to get started with CouchDB, you need to install the CouchDB application. You may be lucky enough to have CouchDB installed already. For example, if you use Ubuntu 9.10 (Karmic) or later, then CouchDB comes pre-installed.

If not, you'll need to use one of the methods below to get CouchDB installed on your system:

- Install using the native packages for your chosen Linux platform. Many of the Linux distributions include CouchDB within their standard package suites.
- By downloading the source code from the Apache CouchDB project page. Building from source requires a suitable build environment, some libraries, and prerequisites (such as Erlang). In general this method is not recommended as the prebuilt packages are much easier to use.

The first method is the easiest solution and will get you up and running as quickly as possible. The latter option may be useful to you if you want to do any development or customization of CouchDB.

Installation on Linux

Certain Linux platforms either include CouchDB or provide a package as part of its native package management system.

On Ubuntu and Debian you can use:

```
sudo aptitude install couchdb
```

On Gentoo Linux there is a CouchDB ebuild available:

```
sudo emerge couchdb
```

In all cases, the installation should install and automatically start CouchDB for you. If not, you can always start or stop using the init scripts. For example:

```
/etc/init.d/couchdb start
```

Installation on Mac OS X

On Max OS X there are builds available using Homebrew (see *http://github.com/mxcl/ homebrew*) and MacPorts (see *http://www.macports.org/install.php*). Both of these packages are based on the native Apache CouchDB release.

You can also find a ready-to-use installation, CouchDBX, that does not require the command-line process of HomeBrew or MacPorts. You can download the CouchDBX package here *http://janl.github.com/couchdbx/*.

Using Homebrew

To install using Homebrew, in a Terminal type:

```
brew install couchdb
```

CouchDB can then be started using *couchdb*:

```
couchdb
```

Use the -h command-line option to get additional options. You can also set up CouchDB to be started automatically during login.

Using MacPorts

If you use MacPorts then you will already be aware of how easy it is to install a number of open source packages into your system. MacPorts will install both CouchDB and any required packages into your system.

To install CouchDB for the first time, including any dependencies:

```
sudo port install couchdb
```

If you have CouchDB dependencies already installed, MacPorts may not upgrade them for you automatically, this can lead to problems with the running system. To upgrade the packages and install, use:

```
sudo port upgrade couchdb
```

To start CouchDB, you can call it on the command line. If you want to start automatically when your machine starts you can use Mac OS X launch controller mechanism:

```
sudo launchctl load -w /opt/local/Library/LaunchDaemons/org.apache.couchdb.plist
```

This will load and start CouchDB for you, and will automatically start and stop CouchDB when you restart, shutdown, and boot your machine.

Installation on Windows

There are no official Windows builds of CouchDB, but a number of developers are providing different built versions of CouchDB on Windows. The recommended solution is the current beta project for a CouchDB installer.

The Windows Binary Installer (*http://wiki.apache.org/couchdb/Windows%20binary %20installer*) is in beta at the time of this writing. CouchDB is provided as a standard installer package. The installed CouchDB can be run both standalone and also as a service.

Installation from Source

As a rule, installation from source should be avoided. Although installing from source is not a complicated process, in general it makes it difficult to update CouchDB when a new version is released. Also, many of the packaged versions of CouchDB either provide a better overall experience, or include extensions (such as GeoCouch) and performance enhancements that may not exist in the standard CouchDB release.

However, if you still want to go ahead and install using the CouchDB source code, you will need the following packages and libraries already installed:

- GNU C/C++ Compiler
- GNU Make
- Erlang OTP (R12B-5 or later)
- ICU
- OpenSSL
- Mozilla Spidermonkey
- libcurl

Once you have installed all of the dependencies, you should download and extract the CouchDB source archive. Within the archive you will need to use the *configure* tool to configure the source code build, specifying everything from the installation location to the location of the various dependent libraries.

Configuring and Building CouchDB

Unless you have specific requirements, *configure* will probably work everything out for you and you can simply run:

```
./configure
```

Once the configuration stage has finished, you should see:

```
You have configured Apache CouchDB, time to relax.
Relax.
```

Now you must build and install the source package using:

```
make && sudo make install
```

You might want to check the *INSTALL* file for more information on configuration and installation.

Running CouchDB

You can start CouchDB by running:

```
couchdb
```

You should avoid running CouchDB as the super user, just in case your installation is compromised. Instead, create a CouchDB user (couchdb) and set the ownership and permissions of the CouchDB database and support files to the configured user. For example:

```
chown -R couchdb:couchdb /usr/local/etc/couchdb
chown -R couchdb:couchdb /usr/local/var/lib/couchdb
chown -R couchdb:couchdb /usr/local/var/log/couchdb
chown -R couchdb:couchdb /usr/local/var/run/couchdb
chmod -R 0770 /usr/local/etc/couchdb
chmod -R 0770 /usr/local/var/lib/couchdb
chmod -R 0770 /usr/local/var/log/couchdb
chmod -R 0770 /usr/local/var/run/couchdb
```

You can now start CouchDB using the new user:

```
sudo -i -u couchdb couchdb -b
```

For more examples of installation and setup, including ways of automatically starting CouchDB, see the *INSTALL* file.

Next Steps

There are a few different things that you might want to try next to ensure that your CouchDB is running correctly and that you can use CouchDB effectively, depending on your environment.

The primary step to try is to access your running CouchDB installation. Depending on your platform and installation type, your browser may have already been opened with the correct link; if not, you can access Futon, the built-in administration interface to CouchDB by going to the URL:

http://127.0.0.1:5984/_utils/index.html

Futon is a web-based interface to the main functionality in CouchDB and provides support for editing the configuration information, creating databases, documents, design documents (and therefore views, shows and lists) and starting and requesting replication.

For the main database operations, your first step should be to select the Create Database item on the home screen. Once your database is created, you can create new documents and from there start creating views and other methods of getting information out of the database.

Futon supports most operations, but the best way to interact with CouchDB is through the HTTP REST interface, which will be the focus of the rest of this book.

By default, your CouchDB installation will listen only on the localhost IP address and port (127.0.0.1:5984). This may cause a problem if you want to use your CouchDB database from a different machine. You can solve this by opening the configuration within Futon (see the links on the right-hand side), and finding the `bind_address` entry. You can change the address to `0.0.0.0`, which will listen on all available interfaces for the specified port of your machine.

To edit this value within Futon, double-click the value, change to the desired IP address, and then click the green tick to the right of the field. Once the value has been updated, restart your CouchDB installation, and your CouchDB server should now be available on the rest of your local network.

Of course, opening up CouchDB in this way means anybody can view it. You may or may not want this, and there is a complete security system built into CouchDB that can help protect your system. A simple step you can take, however, is to restrict the administration controls on your server.

When CouchDB is first set up, it is running in what is called "Admin Party Mode." This means anybody accessing the machine has full adminstration rights (including changing your database and document contents and your configuration). You can switch this off by clicking on the "Fix This" link next to the Admin Party Mode warning in the bottom right of the Futon window.

This will prompt you for a username and password that will be given administration rights. This will protect your system. One downside to this is that using the HTTP REST interface is more complex as you may need to authenticate for certain operations.

With that in mind, let's leap right into the basics of using the HTTP REST interface and how to get data into and out of your database.

CHAPTER 3

CouchDB Basics

Before you start using the CouchDB API, you need to think about the basic processes of accessing the CouchDB server, and how you perform the basic commands and operations that make up your interaction.

For this chapter, we are going to concern ourselves with the basic layout, structure, and how to communicate and exchange the basic information to and from the server.

On that note, it is worth restating that CouchDB works entirely through the HTTP-based CouchDB REST API. That means that if you have an application or environment that can talk HTTP (and many can), you can communicate through the CouchDB API. The interaction is entirely based around the HTTP protocol and the path and data that you supply, either as part of the URL specification or as HTTP payload data.

In this context, HTTP is ideally suited to the database interactions because it supports many of the same basic operations in a database (Create, Retrieve, Update, and Delete) and can be directly mapped to the HTTP protocol operations of PUT, GET, POST, and DELETE.

The URL component of the HTTP request is important within CouchDB in that it is used to identify individual components (databases, documents, other components) within CouchDB. More on this later in the chapter.

Looking at everything without seeing it in action would be difficult, so let's look at some basic interactions that you might typically perform with your CouchDB database.

Using Futon

Futon is a native web-based interface built into CouchDB. It provides a basic interface to the majority of the functionality, including the ability to create, update, delete, and view documents and views, provides access to the configuration parameters, and an interface for initiating replication.

You can do nearly everything that you would need to do with your CouchDB database within Futon, including creating the data, writing the views and design documents, and retrieving the information. Most of the operations within CouchDB are based around the same simple principles of editing documents,

The default view is the Overview page, which provides you with a list of the databases. The basic structure of the page is consistent regardless of the section you are in. The main panel on the left provides the main interface to the databases, configuration, or replication systems. The side panel on the right, as shown in Figure 3-1, provides navigation to the main areas of the Futon interface.

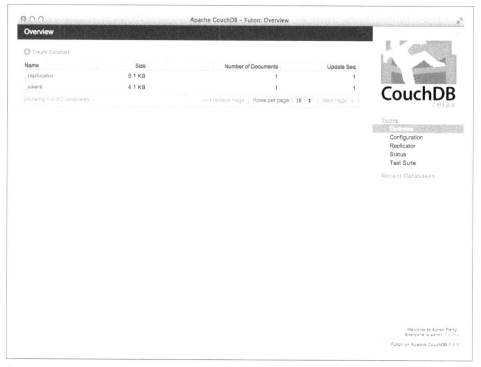

Figure 3-1. Futon Overview

The main sections are:

Overview
> The main overview page, which provides a list of the databases and provides the interface for querying the database and creating and updating documents

Configuration
> An interface into the configuration of your CouchDB installation that allows you to edit the different configurable parameters

Replicator
> An interface to the replication system that enables you to initiate replication between local and remote databases

Status

> Displays a list of the running background tasks on the server, including view index building, compaction, and replication. The *Status* page is an interface to the Active tasks API call.

Verify installation

> Allows you to check whether all of the components of your CouchDB installation are correctly installed

Test suite

> Allows you to run the built-in test suite. This executes a number of test routines entirely within your browser to test the API and functionality of your CouchDB installation. If you select this page, you can run the tests by using the Run All button. This will execute all the tests, which may take some time.

Managing Databases and Documents

You can manage databases and documents within Futon using the main Overview section of the Futon interface.

To create a new database, click the Create Database... button. You will be prompted for the database name, as shown in Figure 3-2.

Figure 3-2. Creating a Database

Once you have created the database (or selected an existing one), you will be shown a list of the current documents. If you create a new document or select an existing document, you will be presented with the edit document display.

Editing documents within Futon requires selecting the document and then editing (and setting) the fields for the document individually before saving the document back into the database.

For example, Figure 3-3 shows the editor for a single document, a newly created document with a single ID, and the document _id field.

Figure 3-3. Editing a Document

To add a field to the document:

1. Click "Add Field".
2. In the field name box, enter the name of the field you want to create. For example, "company".
3. Click the green tick next to the field name to confirm the field name change.
4. Double-click the corresponding Value cell.
5. Enter a company name, for example, "Example".
6. Click the green tick next to the field value to confirm the field value.

7. The document is still not saved at this point. You must explicitly save the document by clicking the Save Document button at the top of the page. This will save the document, and then display the new document with the saved revision information (the _rev field). See Figure 3-4.

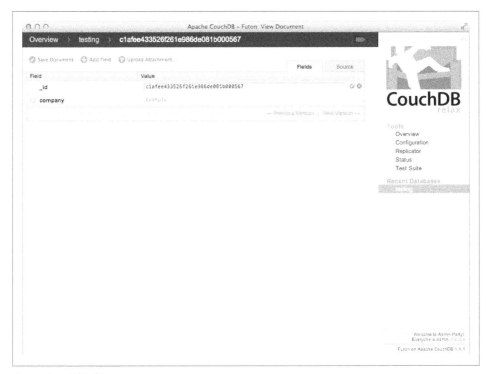

Figure 3-4. Edited Document

The same basic interface is used for all editing operations within Futon. You must remember to save the individual element (fieldname, value) using the green tick button before saving the document.

Configuring Replication

When you click the Replicator option within the Tools menu, you are presented with the Replicator screen. This allows you to start replication between two databases by filling in or selecting the appropriate options within the form provided, shown in Figure 3-5.

To start a replication process, either select the local database or enter a remote database name into the corresponding areas of the form. Replication occurs from the database on the left to the database on the right.

Figure 3-5. Replication Form

If you are specifying a remote database name, you must specify the full URL of the remote database (including the host, port number, and database name). If the remote instance requires authentication, you can specify the username and password as part of the URL, for example, `http://username:pass@remotehost:5984/demo`.

To enable continuous replication, check the Continuous checkbox.

To start the replication process, click Replication. The replication process should start and will continue in the background. If the replication process will take a long time, you can monitor the status of the replication using the Status option under the Tools menu.

Once replication has been completed, the page will show the information returned when the replication process completes by the API.

The Replicator tool is an interface to the underlying replication API.

Populating a Simple Database

There are many potential ways to interact with CouchDB, but probably the easiest to use is the *curl* command-line tool. This is really useful because the interaction is about as raw as it gets. You can see the HTTP interface, the basics of the operations, and the structure and format of the information when it comes back. All of this provides you with a good basic understanding of what is going on when you interact with your server.

Let's get started. Before you can create documents in your database, you need to create a database in which the documents can be stored. Your CouchDB instance can support multiple databases on one system. You should try and keep all of your documents for a single application within one database. There are a number of reasons for this, not least of which is that, internally, CouchDB is unable to access the documents of a different database than the one currently being accessed. For example, you cannot access documents in the database accounts when viewing the database customers. We'll talk a little more about that when we look at document design later in this chapter.

Before creating our first database, we can check if the CouchDB instance is available by accessing the URL for the database using a simple GET request:

```
curl http://127.0.0.1:5984
```

Let's just dissect that request for a second. We haven't specified the request type, so *curl* will send a GET request. The URL is the URL of the CouchDB instance. In this case, we've used the localhost address and the default CouchDB port number, 5984.

This returns the database information. I've formatted in the output below for clarity, but CouchDB outputs this information as one long JSON string, which can be difficult to read. Fortunately, JSON doesn't care about whitespace, and the compact nature of the output keeps the size of the responses down, but isn't very human-readable.:

```
{
    "couchdb" : "Welcome",
    "version" : "1.1.0",
}
```

 For some URLs, especially those that include special characters such as ampersand (&), exclamation mark (!), or question mark (?), you should quote the URL you are specifying on the command line. For example:

```
curl 'http://couchbase:5984/_uuids?count=5'
```

Creating Databases

You can explicitly set the HTTP command using the -X command-line option. When creating a new database, you need to specify the operation as being a PUT. The mnemonic is that we are putting a new database into the system. The PUT operation is idempotent; that is, the content of the URL specifies the name of the object we are creating through the HTTP request. When creating a database, you set the name of the database in the URL you send using a PUT request:

```
curl -X PUT http://192.168.0.57:5984/recipes
{"ok":true}
```

Note the URL structure, the recipes on the end of the URL is the name of the database that we are creating. The response is a standard one from CouchDB, the JSON document returned contains a single field, ok with the value true to indicate that the operation succeeded.

As a small diversion, if you send the command again, you will get an error message telling you that the database already exists:

```
curl -X PUT http://127.0.0.1:5984/recipes
{"error":"file_exists","reason":"The database could not be created, the file already
exists."}
```

Again, this JSON document also has a common structure, a field caled error with the error string, and a field reason with a more detailed description of the issue.

Database names are limited to the following:

- Lowercase characters (a-z)
- Name must begin with a lowercase letter
- Digits (0-9)
- Any of the characters _, $, (,), +, -, and /

Now that we have created the database, we can retrieve the database information by submitting a GET request to the same URL. The output here is formatted again for clarity:

```
curl -X GET http://192.168.0.57:5984/recipes
{
    "compact_running" : false,
    "doc_count" : 0,
    "db_name" : "recipes",
    "purge_seq" : 0,
    "committed_update_seq" : 0,
    "doc_del_count" : 0,
    "disk_format_version" : 5,
    "update_seq" : 0,
    "instance_start_time" : "1306421773496000",
    "disk_size" : 79
}
```

The information returned here is beyond the current information we need, but if the information is returned, then the database must exist.

Creating Documents

Now that we have a database, we can create a document. To do that, you need to submit payload data; that is, data in the body of the HTTP request using the -d option to *curl*. When creating a document, the payload is the document that we want to add to the database:

```
curl -H 'Content-type: application/json' \
    -X POST http://192.168.0.57:5984/recipes \
    -d '{"title": "Lasagne"}'
{"ok":true,
 "id":"8843faaf0b831d364278331bc3001bd8",
 "rev":"1-33b9fbce46930280dab37d672bbc8bb9"}
```

In the above example, the argument after the -d option is the JSON of the document
we want to submit, in this case a placeholder for a recipe. Note here that we did a POST.
Within CouchDB, a POST creates a new document with a document ID automatically
generated by CouchDB. This is the ID field in the returned JSON structure.

Also included in the returned JSON structure is the revision ID. Revisions are important
in CouchDB. You cannot update a document in the database without knowing the
current revision of the document. This is a failsafe to ensure that you do not just over-
write the document with a new version. You have to update the document using the
revision ID and document ID. If the revision that you supply is wrong, the update will
fail. Revisions are also used in other parts of the system. The replication system makes
use of the revision so that the differences between documents on the two databases can
be compared and used as the content.

Of course, now that we've added the document to the database, we might want to get
it back again. The operation is a GET (we are retrieving the document) and we need to
specify the document ID as part of the URL:

```
curl -X GET http://192.168.0.57:5984/recipes/8843faaf0b831d364278331bc3001bd8
{"_id":"8843faaf0b831d364278331bc3001bd8",
 "_rev":"1-33b9fbce46930280dab37d672bbc8bb9",
 "title":"Lasagne"}
```

Let's decode that URL again. The first part of the path is the name of the database that
we created, recipes. The second component is the document ID that we were given
when the document was created under CouchDB. This document ID is slightly ugly,
but it works just a reference so that you can get the document back. Ordinarily you
probably wouldn't use this ID directly, but you might determine the ID from a view
index request, and then use the document ID to get the full document from the database. We'll look at views in Chapter 4.

The document ID itself is just a string. There are times when you might want to create
a document with an ID that you do know or that does have some significance. You can
do this by using a PUT request. Remember when we created a database, and we stated
the name of the database as part of the URL? We can do the same with a document. If
you PUT the document and specify the document name as part of the URL, then the
path component becomes the document ID. Let's demonstrate that with an example:

```
curl -H 'Content-type: application/json' \
    -X PUT \
    http://127.0.0.1:5984/recipes/lasagne \
    -d '{"title": "Lasagne"}'
{"ok":true,"id":"lasagne","rev":"1-f07d272c69ca1ba91b94544ec8eda1b6"}
```

This time we specified the URL path as /recipes/lasagne, the first part is the database name, and the second part is the document name. Because we used PUT we created a document with the URL path specified.

Updating Documents

Now that we've created the record, we can update it by using PUT with the new document data and supplying the revision number to verify that we are updating the document that we think we are updating. Updating the document is a case of sending the new JSON for the document:

```
curl -H 'Content-type: application/json' \
    -X PUT http://127.0.0.1:5984/recipes/lasagne \
    -d '{"title": "Lasagne al Forno", "_rev": "1-f07d272c69ca1ba91b94544ec8eda1b6"}'
{"ok":true,"id":"lasagne","rev":"2-77b8d2ee630bd017122ea2fe0b10a8b4"}
```

There are a few things going on here, so let's list them out to be clear:

- The URL contains the full path to the document (that is DATABASE/DOCID). We know now the document that we are updating, so we must reference it explicitly as the document to be affected by the update.

- PUT is being used because now the document has been created, we have a URL that refers directly to that document. Think of it in the same way as you would editing a file on your machine. Until the file is saved with a filename, you can't edit the contents, only change the contents of the unsaved document. But once we know the name (document ID), we know where to send the updates.

- Updating the document means updating the entire document. You cannot add a field to an existing document. You can only write an entirely new version of the document into the database with the same document ID. Again, think of the file analogy. You can only change the contents of the document by opening it, updating the documents, and saving it back.

- We've supplied the revision number as part of the JSON of the request. Note that the revision ID (rev) is prefixed with an underscore. This is to differentiate the field from a valid field in the document. The entire revision ID must be quoted in its entirety.

The returned JSON contains the success message, the ID of the document being updated (even though we know that already), and the new revision information. If we wanted to update the new version of the document that we just saved into the database, we would need to quote this new revision number.

Deleting Documents

Now we've created a document and updated it, what if we want to delete it? The DELETE HTTP command can do that for us, and since we know the document ID, we can guess that the operation will be similar to the following:

```
curl -H 'Content-type: application/json'
    -X DELETE
    http://127.0.0.1:5984/recipes/lasagne
{"error":"conflict","reason":"Document update conflict."}
```

Whoa! That failed. Why? Because we've tried to delete the document without telling CouchDB that we know what the current revision is. The failsafe is acting again to ensure that we don't just blindly delete a document that we think we know about. We can supply the revision ID as part of the URL submission:

```
curl -H 'Content-type: application/json' \
    -X DELETE \
    http://127.0.0.1:5984/recipes/lasagne?rev=2-77b8d2ee630bd017122ea2fe0b10a8b4
{"ok":true,"id":"lasagne","rev":"3-3ba3659cc3189cc87bb070cf5568ea39"}
```

Success! Note that we have been given a new revision. Thought you were deleting the document, right? The revision in this instance is also there because when replicating documents we need to know that a document has been deleted. You can verify that the document is deleted by doing a GET:

```
curl -H 'Content-type: application/json'
    -X GET
    http://127.0.0.1:5984/recipes/lasagne
{"error":"not_found","reason":"deleted"}
```

So it is deleted. We'll return to the significance and roles of revision again when looking deeper at the revision system in CouchDB.

Deleting Databases

As a final step, and just to clean up after ourselves, let's delete the database that we created:

```
curl -X DELETE http://127.0.0.1:5984/recipes
{"ok":true}
```

Note we didn't need any confirmation for that. Without any type of security in place, anybody can delete the database. Also note that there are no revision IDs for the database as a whole. It is just a container for the documents that we want to store.

Common Operations

The sequence of operations that have been demonstrated in the preceding section are used throughout the entire scope of interactions within CouchDB. The basic CouchDB document operations are detailed above. The same operations are used to upload attachments to documents and to create and update design documents, which are the main two additional interactions you will experience with CouchDB for the purposes of creating and updating material.

Now that you have the basics, let's take a closer look at some of the specifics surrounding these operations and how the inner workings of the HTTP protocol and URL systems within CouchDB operate.

HTTP Operations

All of your interactions with CouchDB will be through HTTP. HTTP is an open standard that is well-defined and well-represented. It is also very simple and straightforward in nature. We don't need to go into the details of HTTP, but we can look at some of the key details.

The main element of HTTP is the method. Most people are familiar with the GET, POST, and PUT if they have done any kind of web programming, but there are a few other operations such as HEAD and DELETE that are useful when talking to CouchDB. With CouchDB, most of them have significance in the operation and their functionality:

GET

> Request the specified database, document, design document, or other object or functionality. As with normal HTTP requests, the format of the URL defines what is returned. With CouchDB, this can include static items, database documents, and configuration and statistical information. In most cases, the information is returned in the form of a JSON document.

HEAD

> The HEAD method is used to get the HTTP header of a GET request without the body of the response. Within CouchDB, the primary use case is when you want to get the information about a document without retrieving the document itself. The HEAD method returns metadata about the document or other object being accessed within the HTTP headers returned.

POST

> Upload or send data. Within CouchDB, POST is used to set values, including uploading documents, setting document values, and starting certain administration commands. The POST method is used when you don't know the ID of the object being accessed, or are using an implied ID. For example, when creating a document when you want CouchDB to generate the ID for you.

PUT

> Used to put a specified resource with a specified ID or other identifier. For example, you can explicitly create a document with a given ID by using PUT and a URL with the document ID. In CouchDB, PUT is used to create new objects, including databases, documents, views, and design documents.

DELETE

> Deletes the specified resource, including documents, views, and design documents.

COPY

A special method that can be used to copy documents and objects. The COPY method is not an HTTP standard, but it is supported by CouchDB as a way of duplicating information.

Errors

The HTTP standards also include a series of error numbers. These are well-defined and understood (everybody must have come across a "404: resource not found" error while browsing the Internet). The benefit of the numbered errors is that they are easy to understand and cope with, and because they come back with the header, they are easy to identify without a heavy overhead. For completeness, CouchDB also includes a JSON error string for many of the operations so that you can get a CouchDB-specific error.

A sample of the main error codes are listed below. This is not an exhaustive list, but merely designed to show the main errors that you might get back:

200 - OK
Request completed successfully.

201 - Created
Document created successfully.

202 - Accepted
Request has been accepted, but the corresponding operation may not have completed. This is used for background operations, such as database compaction.

404 - Not Found
The requested content could not be found. The content will include further information, as a JSON object, if available. The structure will contain two keys, error and reason. For example:

    {"error":"not_found","reason":"no_db_file"}

405 - Resource Not Allowed
A request was made using an invalid HTTP request type for the URL requested. For example, you have requested a PUT when a POST is required. Errors of this type can also be triggered by invalid URL strings.

409 - Conflict
Request resulted in an update conflict.

415 - Bad Content Type
The content types supported and the content type of the information being requested or submitted indicate that the content type is not supported.

500 - Internal Server Error
The request was invalid, either because the supplied JSON was invalid, or invalid information was supplied as part of the request.

HTTP Headers

Because CouchDB uses HTTP for all communication, you need to ensure that the correct HTTP headers are supplied (and processed on retrieval) so that you get the right format and encoding. Different environments and clients will be more or less strict on the effect of these HTTP headers (especially when not present). Where possible, you should be as specific as you can.

Request Headers

Content-type

> Specifies the content type of the information being supplied within the request. The specification uses MIME type specifications. For the majority of requests this will be JSON (application/json). For some settings, the MIME type will be plain text. When uploading attachments, it should be the corresponding MIME type for the attachment or binary (application/octet-stream).
>
> The use of the Content-type on a request is highly recommended.

Accept

> Specifies the list of accepted data types to be returned by the server (i.e., that are accepted/understandable by the client). The format should be a list of one or more MIME types, separated by colons.
>
> For the majority of requests, the definition should be for JSON data (application/json). For attachments, you can either specify the MIME type explicitly or use */* to specify that all file types are supported. If the Accept header is not supplied, then the */* MIME type is assumed (i.e., client accepts all formats).
>
> The use of Accept in queries for CouchDB is not required, but is highly recommended as it helps to ensure that the data returned can be processed by the client.
>
> If you specify a data type using the Accept header, CouchDB will honor the specified type in the Content-type header field returned. For example, if you explicitly request application/json in the Accept of a request, the returned HTTP headers will use the value in the returned Content-type field.
>
> For example, when sending a request without an explicit Accept header, or when specifying */*:
>
> ```
> GET /recipes HTTP/1.1
> Host: couchbase:5984
> Accept: */*
> ```
>
> The returned headers are:
>
> ```
> Server: CouchDB/1.0.1 (Erlang OTP/R13B)
> Date: Thu, 13 Jan 2011 13:39:34 GMT
> Content-Type: text/plain;charset=utf-8
> Content-Length: 227
> Cache-Control: must-revalidate
> ```

Note that the returned content type is `text/plain` even though the information returned by the request is in JSON format.

Explicitly specifying the `Accept` header:

```
GET /recipes HTTP/1.1
Host: couchbase:5984
Accept: application/json
```

The headers returned include the `application/json` content type:

```
Server: CouchDB/1.0.1 (Erlang OTP/R13B)
Date: Thu, 13 Jan 2011 13:40:11 GMT
Content-Type: application/json
Content-Length: 227
Cache-Control: must-revalidate
```

Response Headers

Response headers are returned by the server when sending back content and include a number of different header fields, many of which are standard HTTP response header and have no significance to CouchDB operation. The list of response headers important to CouchDB are listed below:

Content-type
: Specifies the MIME type of the returned data. For most requests, the returned MIME type is `text/plain`. All text is encoded in Unicode (UTF-8), and this is explicitly stated in the returned `Content-type`, as `text/plain;charset=utf-8`.

Cache-control
: The cache control HTTP response header provides a suggestion for client caching mechanisms on how to treat the returned information. CouchDB typically returns the `must-revalidate`, which indicates that the information should be revalidated if possible. This is used to ensure that the dynamic nature of the content is correctly updated.

Content-length
: The length (in bytes) of the returned content.

Etag
: The `Etag` HTTP header field is used to show the revision for a document.

HTTP URL Paths

Because of the REST interface and the idempotency of the URLs that you use with CouchDB, the URLs that you use are significant and important. They define not only the components you are accessing, but in some areas of the system, they specify the ID of the object that you are creating.

The structure for the URLs has been standardized, and you should be able to both look at a URL that you are using to understand what it does, and to construct one to access the information that you want.

There are some conventions:

- Components prefixed with an underscore always access some internal system or function. For example, when accessing /_uuids, you get a list of UUIDs from the system. Where the underscore prefix is used on a value at the start of the URL, then the special functionality is part of the entire system.

- Except as noted above, the first component of the path is the database name. From now on, all the operations are directly related to the specified database.

- If a second component starts with an underscore, now the specified operation is also special and unique to that database. For example, the compaction operation is specific to a database.

  Other operations that fall into this group are accessing design documents (which output views and other information) and retrieving information from views and other dynamic content.

- If the second component does not contain an underscore then it is treated as a document name. All further path elements relate to the document (such as an attachment).

These rules are very simplistic, but they do allow you to determine an operation and their effect by looking at the URL. For example:

URL	Operation
PUT /db	Create a new database
GET /db	Get the database information
PUT /db/document	Create a document with the specified ID within the specified database; or update an existing document
GET /db/document	Get the document
DELETE /db/document	Delete the specified document from the specified database
GET /db/_design/design-doc	Get the design document definition
GET /db/_design/design-doc/_view/view-name	Access the view view-name from the design document design-doc from the specified database

This is by no means an exhaustive list. There are over 100 different URL forms used to create, access, and manage content and operations within CouchDB.

JSON

CouchDB consumes and returns complex data structures in the JavaScript Object Notation (JSON) format. JSON is a very simple and straightforward format that is easy to create, produce, and understand. It also works very simply with other languages and it's easy to convert between the internal representations of languages like Python or Java to and from the JSON format.

The most useful aspect of JSON is that, as a native JavaScript format, it works well with the JavaScript engine embedded into CouchDb and used for much of the internal functionality. Furthermore, as a database designed to be used in web application development, speaking JSON as a native data structure format enables easy exchange of data with web applications that can consume and generate JSON formatted data.

JSON supports the same basic types as supported by JavaScript:

Number
> Either integer or floating-point

String
> This should be enclosed by double quotes and supports Unicode characters and backslash escaping. For example:

```
"A String"
```

Boolean
> A true or false value. You can use these strings directly. For example:

```
{ "value": true}
```

Array
> A list of values enclosed in square brackets. For example:

```
["one", "two", "three"]
```

Object
> A set of key/value pairs (i.e., an associative array or hash). The key must be a string, but the value can be any of the supported JSON values. For example:

```
{
    "servings" : 4,
    "subtitle" : "Easy to make in advance, and then cook when ready",
    "cooktime" : 60,
    "title" : "Chicken Coriander"
}
```

JSON is used in other places within CouchDB. All of the data and meta-information generated by CouchDB and internal elements such as the configuration information are all generated as JSON.

The indexing system and views are also generated as a JSON structure and the design document, which forms a key part of the application functionality within CouchDB, is defined using JSON.

Documents

Now that we've looked at how to create and update documents within the database, it's time to take a quick look and reflect on both the structure of your documents and the content of the collection of documents all in one database.

There are three main areas to the consider: the basic document structure (fields and field types), the use of document types to track different document structures, and the structure and consistency of the documents that you store.

Document Structure

The document approach requires some careful consideration when it comes to formatting and using your data. The main consideration is that because you can put all of the information about a single item into one document, you need a structure that is capable of defining and displaying that information. JSON is very flexible, but keep in mind that you also want to easily process the information.

Just like in a database that requires a schema, there are some conventions and field types that you should consider including in your documents.

Some good habits to get into:

- Don't store a separate ID or reference; use the document ID as the unique identifier. The exception to this rule, of course, is if you have a separate identifier (such as a product code, ISBN, or other information) that you want to use in addition to your main document ID because it provides reference or connectivity information.

- Consider using a type to identify different document types. See the next section for more information.

- Use fields to store the document data, and use compound fields to store related information. For example, if you are modeling a blog post system, store the blog data as top-level fields in the document and comments as a compound element:

```
{
    "title": "My Blog Post",
    "comments": [
        {
            "from": "Joe Blog",
            "comment": "Good post!",
        }
    ]
}
```

- Remember to include standard fields such as timestamps (created, updated), and status so that you can organize and identify the content.
- Use arrays for lists of values. Sounds obvious, but within a document database, the temptation can be to create a completely flat structure. A typical example is tags, often used to classify data:

```
{
    "tags" : ["blog", "article", "computing"]
}
```

- Don't concatenate values because you can, but use a compound value to hold the information. For example, when listing ingredients within a recipe, the temptation is to put the full ingredient—2 cups carrots—into a single field within your document. When you come to extract or search on that information, you will probably want the carrots more than the measurement. Instead, store it as a compound value:

```
[
    {
        "ingredient": "butter",
        "measure": "50 g"
    },
    {
        "ingredient": "onion",
        "measure": "1"
    },
    ...
]
```

- Don't rely on the implied field sequence of the document. For example, don't assume that if you create the document with three fields—title, author, and description—that the fields will be stored or returned in that order.

  This doesn't affect top-level fields so much since you can access them by name, but it does affect compound values. If you want to retain a specific order, use an array of compound values, as in the previous ingredient example.

- When thinking about your data structure, decide on whether you want to use one document that contains all of the information or multiple documents that you will later combine together with a clever view.

  Using the blog post as an example, you can put the blog and comments into one document, or the blog content in one and the individual comments in further documents (one per comment).

  The main consideration is how frequently you expect to update the information. If the blog and comments are one document, the entire document will need to be retrieved, updated with the new comment, and then saved back. If the blog and comments are separate documents, all you need do is another document with the comment content.

Document Types

Databases are used to define entire collections of information. For some databases, all of your documents will be the same type and contain the same information and probably share a common (if not identical) structure.

But within CouchDB, you have to remember that you can only access one database at a time. You cannot produce a view over more than one database, nor can you refer or access a document from another database when accessing a document from a different database.

The best solution to this problem, that also helps ensure consistency and structure, is to use a field called type or schema that identifies what the document contains. For example, in a blog enviroment you might store the blog posts and comments separately, so a blog post would like this:

```
{
    "title": "My Blog Post",
    "created_at": "2011-11-27T14:34",
    "content" : "My first blog post"
    "author" : "MC Brown",
    "schema" : "blogpost",
}
```

A comment is identified (and formatted) differently:

```
{
    "schema": "comment",
    "blogdocid": "myblogpost",
    "from": "Joe Blog",
    "comment": "Good post!",
}
```

When writing views and searching and referring the content, the type or schema field can be used to identify the different document types and create different views and representations of the information accordingly.

Structure and Consistency

There are no constraints or schemas for a document database, but that doesn't mean that you can ignore aspects like the simplicity and consistency of the format. For example, there's no point in using a field for the title of a recipe if in one document the field name is title, recipetitle in another, and recipe_name in others.

It is a good idea to employ some basic consistency in your field names and contents to ensure you can cope with future changes and updates. I tend to use the same field names for all sorts of different data types across many different databases.

A good tip here is to store and use a sample document that contains the basic document structure, which you can then use as a template or reference for your other documents.

You can also use document validation (a component of the design document) to either check or control and update the structure and consistency of the documents as they are saved and updated in the database.

CHAPTER 4

Design Documents

In Chapter 3, we examined the basics of creating documents in a CouchDB database. Documents are where you store the data, but the only way to get the information back out from your documents is to know the document ID you used to store the document. There are a few different issues with the document structure that you may want to consider, such as enforcing document structure, handling document validation, and searching and querying the document data.

The key to all of these different types of information, and many others, is the design document. Aside from the core document storage, the design document is probably the most important component of your CouchDB database. Design documents contain all of the database logic about the document you are storing. Think of the design document as the glue that turns each of your documents into the format or structure that you need for your application.

The different components of your design document are written using JavaScript and they are executed within the CouchDB application. Because they are code, you can perform almost any action that would perform with JavaScript on an object. This means that you can select fields and components, perform test, reformat, calculate, and many other operations. This is useful as the different components of the design document work together to support the different formatting, indexing, and other procedures.

To be more specific, a design document provides the following:

Views

> Views are functions that take your document data and produce searchable lists of information based on the document's contents. Views are incredibly simple yet also very powerful and provide the main route of entry into your data for information for which you don't know the document ID.

Shows

> A show converts a single document into another format, usually HTML, although you can output the document in any format, including JSON or XML, to suit your

application. Shows can also be used to simplify the JSON content of a document into a simpler or reduced format.

Lists

A list is to a view (or collection of documents) as a show is to a single document. You can use a list to format the view as an HTML table, or a page of information or as XML of your document collection. In this way, a list acts as a transform on the entire content on the view into another format.

Document validation

Because you can store any JSON document in your database, one of the issues is maintaining consistency. This is what the document validation functions solve. When you save a document into CouchDB, the validation function is called, and it can either check or even reformat the incoming document to meet your requirements and standards for different documents.

Update handlers

Update handlers can be used to perform an action on a document when the document is updated. Unlike document validation, update handlers are explicitly called, but they can be used to make changes to a document within the server without having to retrieve the document, change it, and save it back (as would be required for a client process). For example, you can use update handlers to increment values in a document, or add and update timestamps.

Filters

When exchanging information between CouchDB databases when using replication or the changes feed, you may want to filter the content of the database. For example, if you store information about your CD and DVD collection in a single database, you may want to exchange only the CD records with another database. This is what a filter function is for: when called, it examines the list of supplied documents from the replication or changes feed and then either returns the document or null.

Design documents are basically just like any other document within a CouchDB database; that is, a JSON structure that you can create and update using the same PUT and POST HTTP operations. The difference is that they are located within a special area of each database (_design), and they are processed and accessed differently when you want to actually execute the functional components.

It's also worth pointing out at this stage that any database can have zero or more design documents. There are no limits to the number of design documents that you have, although from a practical perspective it's unlikely that you'll have more than 10 for most databases, especially since for many of the design document components you can have more than one definition in each design document.

For the moment, we will examine how to create and update design documents, followed by the three main areas of design document functionality, shows, views, and lists.

For some of the examples in this chapter we're going to be working with a database of recipes. The document data contains recipe data, cooking times, ingredient lists, method lists, and keywords. An example of the recipe document for Beef In Red Wine is shown below:

```
{
    "_id": "Beefinredwine",
    "_rev": "1-7098492ad814129ea8f026267a12650b",
    "preptime": "15",
    "servings": "4",
    "keywords": [
        "diet@peanut-free",
        "main ingredient@meat.beef",
        "special collections@cheffy recommended",
        "diet@corn-free",
        "special collections@weekend meal",
        "occasion@entertaining",
        "diet@citrus-free",
        "special collections@very easy",
        "diet@shellfish-free",
        "meal type@main.stews, casseroles, curries",
        "cuisine@european.french",
        "cook method.hob, oven, grill@hob / oven",
        "special collections@basic cooking",
        "diet@egg-free",
        "occasion@prepare-ahead entertaining"
    ],
    "subtitle": "Beef and mushrooms in a rich and warming casserole.",
    "totaltime": "144",
    "cooktime": "129",
    "ingredients": [
        {
            "ingredient": "red wine",
            "measure": "450 ml"
        },
        {
            "ingredient": "pickling onions",
            "measure": "225 g"
        },
        {
            "ingredient": "garlic",
            "measure": "1"
        },
        {
            "ingredient": "bay leaf",
            "measure": "1"
        },
        {
            "ingredient": "beef braising steak",
            "measure": "450 g"
        },
        {
            "ingredient": "rindless streaky bacon",
            "measure": "4 rashers"
        },
```

```
        {
            "ingredient": "plain flour",
            "measure": "25 g"
        },
        {

            "ingredient": "vegetable oil",
            "measure": "3 tsp"
        },
        {

            "ingredient": "button mushrooms",
            "measure": "225 g"
        },
        {

            "ingredient": "butter",
            "measure": "15 g"
        },
        {

            "ingredient": "seasoning",
            "measure": ""
        }
    ],
    "method": [
        {
            "step": "1",
            "text": "Preheat oven to 180°C."
        },
        {
            "step": "2",
            "text": "Melt the butter and oil in a large heatproof ovenproof casserole.
Add the onions. Fry for 2-3 min or until well browned. Remove from pan with a slotted
spoon. Set aside. Keep warm."
        },
        {
            "step": "3",
            "text": "Add the garlic, braising steak and bacon to the pan. Fry for 5 min,
stirring frequently until well browned. Remove from the pan with a slotted spoon. Set
aside with the onions."
        },
        {
            "step": "4",
            "text": "Add the flour to the pan. Cook, stirring, for 1 min. Gradually add
the red wine, stirring frequently until all is incorporated. Bring to the boil."
        },
        {
            "step": "5",
            "text": "Return the onion and meats to the pan with the mushrooms, bay leaf
and seasoning. Return to the boil. "
        },
        {
            "step": "6",
            "text": "Place in oven and cook for 1 hour 30 min until beef is tender."
        }
    ],
    "title": "Beef in red wine"
}
```

Creating Design Documents

The basic format of the design document is a JSON document with a field for each of the major content types (view, list, shows). Depending on the type, the definition then contains one or more further definitions. For example, you can define more than one view in a single design document. Let's have a look at a sample design document to make that clearer:

```
{
    "language": "javascript",
    "views": {
        "all": {
            "map": "function(doc) { emit(doc.title, doc) }",
        },
        "by_title": {
            "map": "function(doc) { if (doc.title != null) emit(doc.title, doc) }",
        },
        "by_keyword": {
            "map": "function(doc) { for(i=0;i<doc.keywords.lenghth();i++)
{ emit(doc.keywords[i], doc); } }",
        },
    },
    "shows": {
        "recipe": "function(doc, req) { return '<h1>' + doc.title + '</h1>' }"
}
```

The above example provides a simple design document that defines three views (more in a moment) and a single show. You can see the structure here with the views collected together, with a single view, such as **by_title**, being defined individually. Similarly, the one show, **recipe**, is part of the **shows** block.

> Technically, CouchDB supports design documents written in languages other than the default embedded JavaScript. You can, for example, use Erlang (the native language used to build CouchDB itself), or indeed any language providing CouchDB is configured correctly. For simplicity, we'll use JavaScript for our examples.

You can save this document into a file and then upload this to the CouchDB design documents area of the recipe database using the same methods as you would for a typical document. The difference is in the document ID. All design documents are located within the **_design** section of the database. They must also have a fixed name; unlike standard documents, you cannot let CouchDB name the design document for you. That means that when creating the document, you must use a PUT request. For example, using curl, you would use:

```
curl -X PUT -d @recipes_view.js 'http://localhost:5984/recipes/_design/recipes'
```

The @ tells curl to load the data from a file (*recipes_view.js*). The URL used specifies the design document area of the database recipes, here calling the design document itself recipes, too.

Now that the design document has been created, you could access all of the different operations (views and shows in this case). There's nothing you need to do to enable or start the functions from working. Once the design document has been uploaded, CouchDB can start making use of it.

The remainder of the interaction with the design document definition is the same as with a standard document. You can retrieve the design document definition by doing a GET on the design document URL:

```
curl -X GET 'http://localhost:5984/recipes/_design/recipes'
{
    "views" : {
        "by_keyword" : {
            "map" : "function(doc) { for(i=0;i<doc.keywords.lenghth();i++)
{ emit(doc.keywords[i], doc); } }"
        },
        "by_title" : {
            "map" : "function(doc) { if (doc.title != null) emit(doc.title, doc) }"
        },
        "all" : {
            "map" : "function(doc) { emit(doc.title, doc) }"
        }
    },
    "language" : "javascript",
    "_id" : "_design/recipes",
    "_rev" : "1-b41a673ce62351a2c629734d4dc220f9",
    "shows" : {
        "recipe" : "function(doc, req) { return '<h1>' + doc.title + '</h1>' }"
    }
}
```

The JSON returned here is formatted for clarity, but you can see that we get the entire document definition back again, plus the _id and _rev fields automatically added by CouchDB. Note here that the _id field is _design/recipes, the URL path of the design document as it was stored into the system.

The _rev parameter should be familiar. If we want to update the definition of the design document, we need to supply that parameter just as we did when updating a typical document. Updates use PUT, and you must put the current revision into the _rev field of the submitted update. For example:

```
/usr/bin/curl -X PUT -H 'Content-type: application/json' \
    -d '{"_rev":"1-b41a673ce62351a2c629734d4dc220f9"}' \
    'http://localhost:5984/recipes/_design/recipes'
```

This deliberately inserts an empty design document with no definitions just to demonstrate.

Finally, you can delete the design document using the HTTP DELETE operation:

```
curl -X DELETE -H 'Content-type: application/json' \
    'http://localhost:5984/recipes/_design/curlrecipes?
rev=3-2d1bca110ccd7263a9f10c79e0de74a7'
```

As you can see, the main operations are the same as for any other document. The only difference is that the content has some functional basis. Let's start by looking at how shows operate.

Shows

Beyond the basic operations of adding and updating records in the database, the most likely operation on a single stored document is that you will want to display the contents. This is the role of a show. A show takes the content of a document and formats it for output.

Notice the word I used wasn't for "display". Although you can use a show for that, shows can be used to output information in any format you want from the document content. You can choose to output some of the document, all of it, or even restructure the document entirely. Because the output is just a text string, that means you can reformat the content as XML, a tab delimited string, even as a UUencoded string if that is what you need.

As you saw in the earlier examples, a show is just a JavaScript function. The function itself is supplied two arguments, the document requested to be processed by the show, and the request object (part of standard JavaScript) that generated the request.

In reality, that means that a basic definition looks like this:

```
function(doc,req) {
}
```

Anything that the function returns is treated as the output that will be returned to the client. Let's look back at the earlier example recipe, now just looking at the one show:

```
{
    "shows": {
        "recipe" : "function (doc,req) { return '<h1>' + doc.title + '</h1>'}"
    }
}
```

The above will output the title field from the supplied document enclosed in the HTML H1 tag. If you upload this to the server as the design document recipes/_design/ detail then you can access the show (that is, process a document created in the last chapter, Lasagne, using the show definition) using the following URL:

```
GET http://localhost:5984/recipes/_design/detail/_show/recipe/Lasagne
```

The URL bears some scrutiny. The first part is the name of the database, "recipes". The second part states that are access a design document, and the third the name of the design document is detail. Then we specify that we are accessing a show called recipe, and that the document ID of the document that we want to process is called Lasagne.

We can describe that more clearly by using a placeholder URL:

```
http://localhost:5984/DBNAME/_design/DESIGNDOCID/_show/SHOWNAME/DOCID
```

The output from the request should be the document title (Lasagne) embedded in the H1 tags:

```
<h1>Lasagne</h1>
```

This is pretty boring, but this is a JavaScript function, so we can actually output something more detailed. Let's try generating a more traditional looking recipe with an updated function:

```
function(doc, req) {
    var output;

    output = '<h1>' + doc.title + '</h1>';
    output += '<p>' + doc.subtitle + '</p>';
    output   += '<h2>Ingredients</h2><ul>';

    for(i=0;i<doc.ingredients.length;i++) {
        output += '<li>' + doc.ingredients[i].measure + ' ' +
            doc.ingredients[i].ingredient + '</li>';
    }

    output += '</ul><h2>Method</h2><ol>';

    for(i=0;i<doc.method.length;i++) {

        output += '<li>' + doc.method[i].text;
    }

    output += '</ol>';

    return output;
}
```

This will generate a recipe, with the subtitle, and then iterate over the ingredients and method steps to produce a fully displayed recipe, as shown in Figure 4-1.

In this case, the output is assumed by CouchDB to be HTML (i.e., with a content type of **text/html**) and UTF-8 formatting.

This native HTML output is useful, but you can be more explicit. The return can just be a string, but you can also return a JSON object that contains both the returned data and other meta information, such as the HTTP header information so that you can specify the content type. This can be useful if you want to ensure that a document formatted as XML through the show function is correctly reported to the client.

To achieve this, rather than returning a string, you return a JSON structure containing the body and header information:

```
function(doc, req) {
    return {
        'body':'<recipe><title>' + doc.title + '</title></recipe>',
```

```
        'headers' : {
            'Content-type': 'application/xml'
        }
    }
}
```

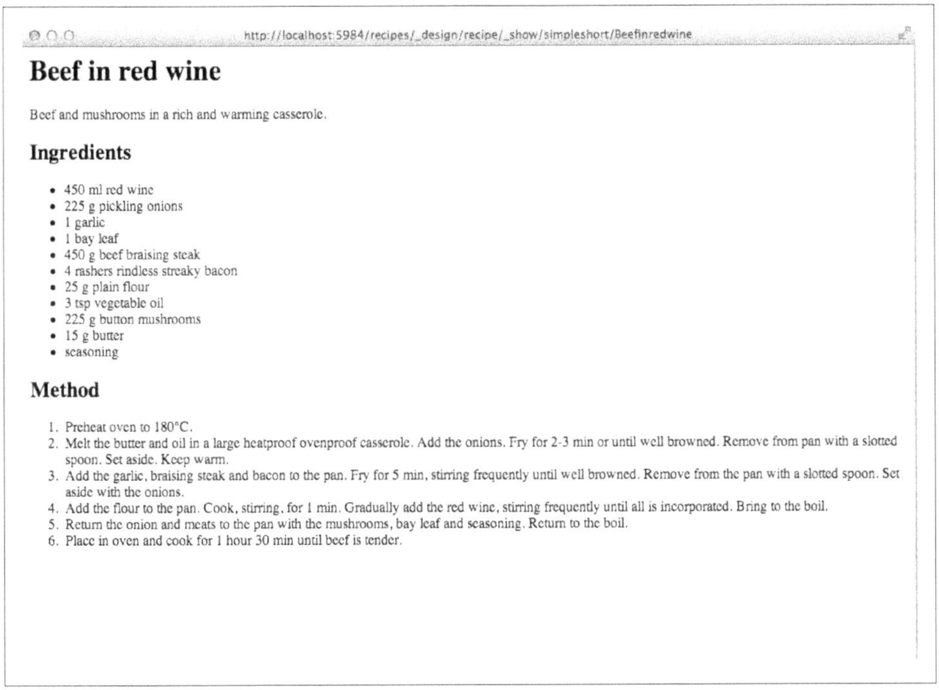

Figure 4-1. Fully displayed Beef in Red Wine recipe

We can put that into the design document as another show:

```
{
    "shows": {
        "recipe": "function(doc, req) { var output; output = '<h1>' + doc.title + '</
h1>'; output += '<p>' + doc.subtitle + '</p>'; output += '<h2>Ingredients</h2><ul>';
for(i=0;i<doc.ingredients.length;i++) { output += '<li>' + doc.ingredients[i].measure
+ ' ' + doc.ingredient\
s[i].ingredient + '</li>';} output += '</ul><h2>Method</h2><ol>';
for(i=0;i<doc.method.length;i++) { output += '<li>' + doc.method[i].text } output +=
'</ol>'; return output; }",
        "asxml": "function(doc, req) { return { 'body':'<recipe><title>' + doc.title
+ '</title></recipe>', 'headers' : {'Content-type': 'application/xml'}}}"
    }
}
```

From a client, you can access the XML version of the document by using the `asxml`
show. For example:

```
GET http://127.0.0.1:5984/recipes/_design/detail/_show/asxml/Beefinredwine
<recipe><title>Beef in red wine</title></recipe>
```

Now you can see how different design documents and their functionality can be grouped together to produce different sets of functionality and information.

The final part of the show functionality is the ability to process the request information. This is the second argument supplied to the show function. The request object contains all of the information about the original request that accessed the show of the document. This includes any HTTP headers, client addresses, and query arguments to the URL request. You can use this information to make decisions about the format or content of the show function. That's beyond the scope of this discussion.

Once you have started using shows, the most common question is how you get another document so that it can be included in the output. You can't. However, you can access multiple documents and then produce multiple outputs of this information. To start doing that, you need to understand views.

Views

Up to now we've made some assumptions about how you want to use the information in your database. Primarily, we've discussed how to store information in the database using a document ID, how to update and manipulate that document, and how to use shows.

To search and aggregate information stored within your CouchDB database, you need to write a view. Views convert the individual documents in your database into a list of information. From that list, you can query and select information from the view, and search and find groups and individual documents.

A view does exactly what the name suggests: it creates a view on your data. That makes it sound incredibly simple, and in fact it really is, but the simplicity also gives the whole process a lot of power.

In fact, views form the basis of a number of key elements of the way CouchDB displays, sorts, and searches information. The main uses of views are:

- Indexing and querying information stored in your documents
- Producing lists of data on specific elements of a document
- Producing tables and lists of information summarizing document data
- Extracting or filtering information from your documents
- Calculating, summarizing, or reducing large numbers of documents

Views are designed within the views section of your design document. You can create multiple views and multiple design documents to create different views and summaries of your information.

View Basics

The first thing you need to know about views is that creating a view also creates an index. The contents of the index are made up of the information that the view generates. The index is in the form of a B-Tree index, which in turn makes the process of retrieving information very quick. How the information in the index is created is determined by the view definition.

The view definition consists of two Javascript functions, the map function, and the reduce function. Therefore, CouchDB supports map/reduce. Map/reduce systems have become popular recently because they allow for very large quantities of information to be processed (and reduced) very quickly and efficiently into the information you need. For the moment, let's concentrate on the map function.

When you create a view, every document in your database is sent to the map function, which is primarily responsible for mapping the information stored within each document into the generated view content. This is composed of three parts: the document ID from which the row of output was generated, the key (which we can use to query and retrieve information), and the value. All of this information is stored in the index, allowing you to very quickly retrieve specific information stored in your database without having to individually load documents.

Let's have a look at a sample map function to process our recipe content:

```
function(doc) {
    if (doc.title != null)
        emit(doc.title, null)
}
```

Let's dissect that function just a little. The function takes a single argument, the document being supplied. Remember, a view is generated by CouchDB, sending each document in the database to the view.

The embedded `if` checks to ensure that we have a valid document. In this case, we're ensuring that the document has a title since this view outputs the recipe by its title.

The `emit()` function is built-in; it generates one row of information from the map function consisting of the key and the value. The key in this case is the document title, and the value null (empty).

Views are defined within the views section of your design document. For example:

```
{
    "views": {
        "by_title": {
            "map": "function(doc) { if (doc.title != null) emit(doc.title, null) }"
        },
    }
}
```

Here our view is called by_title. If the design document is called simple then we can access the view using the following URL:

```
http://127.0.0.1:5984/recipes/_design/simple/_view/by_title
```

The view information generated by this will look similar to the following:

```
{D
    "total_rows" : 2667,
    "rows" : [
        {
            "value" : null,
            "id" : "Aberffrawcake",
            "key" : "Aberffraw cake"
        },
        {
            "value" : null,
            "id" : "Adukiandorangecasserole-microwave",
            "key" : "Aduki and orange casserole - microwave"
        },
        {
            "value" : null,
            "id" : "Aioli-garlicmayonnaise",
            "key" : "Aioli - garlic mayonnaise"
        }
    ],
    "offset" : 0
}
```

The output has been trimmed in this example. You can see that each call to the emit() function has created a single row, containing the implied document ID, key (first argument), and value (second argument).

Accessing a view is significant within CouchDB. To keep the speed of the database when creating and writing documents, the index for a view is not updated when the document is written. This is because, in real terms, this is not the point at which indexing is really useful. The update doesn't need or use the update. Instead, when you access a view, the view is generated and the index is updated.

The first time you access a new view on a database, the entire contents of the database are processed through the view. If you then update, delete, and add new records and access the view again, only the changed documents are updated in the generated index. Obviously if you have a lot of documents in your database then the first time you hit the view, it will take some time to create the index. But the update process is comparatively small.

It's also worth noting that the B-Tree created from a view, and view creation in detail, is tied to the design document. If you define 10 views in your design document then CouchDB will supply each updated document to all 10 views in your design document and update the index, even though you only accessed a single view.

The main benefit of the indexing and B-Tree used for storing the information is that B-Trees are incredibly efficient at pulling out an item based on a single key, or a range of keys, for example, all the recipes from Casserole to Granola.

Querying a View

The information generated by the view can be queried because the generated view has a few properties that may not be immediately obvious. First and foremost, the information output by the view is automatically sorted by its UTF-8 value. You can also specify in the URL that all the view return outputs everything starting from a specific UTF-8 string.

For example, if you wanted to output all of the recipes that have a title starting with "Apricot" then you can use the following URL:

```
http://127.0.0.1:5984/recipes/_design/simple/_view/by_title?startkey=%22Apricot%22
```

Note that the startkey value has to be a JSON value, in this case a quoted string. The generated information is shown below:

```
{"total_rows":2667,"offset":54,"rows":[
{"id":"Apricotandcranberrystuffedlambroll","key":"Apricot and cranberry stuffed lamb
roll","value":null},
{"id":"Apricotandoatcakes","key":"Apricot and oat cakes","value":null},
{"id":"Apricotandoatmealteabread","key":"Apricot and oatmeal tea bread","value":null},
{"id":"Apricotandprunestreuselcake","key":"Apricot and prune streusel
cake","value":null},
{"id":"Apricotcheesecake","key":"Apricot cheesecake","value":null},
{"id":"ApricotChelseabuns","key":"Apricot Chelsea buns","value":null},
{"id":"Apricotcoconuttart","key":"Apricot coconut tart","value":null},
{"id":"ApricotEvespudding","key":"Apricot Eve's pudding","value":null},
{"id":"Apricotfreezerjam","key":"Apricot freezer jam","value":null},
{"id":"Arcticroll","key":"Arctic roll","value":null},
{"id":"Arcticsurprise","key":"Arctic surprise","value":null},
{"id":"Aromaticroastchicken","key":"Aromatic roast chicken","value":null},
...
```

Well, we've found a lot of Apricot recipes, but also some that obviously don't start with Apricot. The reason is that we haven't given a range. We've only specified that the output starts with the specified JSON string.

To do a range we need to specify the endkey. Because in this example we know that the endkey is "Arcticroll", we could specify this in the URL, but we aren't always going to know what the endkey is. If we want to restrict it to those starting with Apricot, we can use the UTF-8 sorting to our advantage. If we add the UTF-8 character 007F to 'Apricot', the range will only include recipes with the title starting with Apricot, even if the document ID contains other characters. Let's see that in action:

```
http://127.0.0.1:5984/recipes/_design/simple/_view/by_title?startkey=%22Apricot
%22&endkey=%22Apricot%007F%22
```

The resulting output contains exactly what we need:

```
{"total_rows":2667,"offset":54,"rows":[
{"id":"Apricotandcranberrystuffedlambroll","key":"Apricot and cranberry stuffed lamb
roll","value":null},
{"id":"Apricotandoatcakes","key":"Apricot and oat cakes","value":null},
{"id":"Apricotandoatmealteabread","key":"Apricot and oatmeal tea bread","value":null},
{"id":"Apricotandprunestreuselcake","key":"Apricot and prune streusel
cake","value":null},
{"id":"Apricotcheesecake","key":"Apricot cheesecake","value":null},
{"id":"ApricotChelseabuns","key":"Apricot Chelsea buns","value":null},
{"id":"Apricotcoconuttart","key":"Apricot coconut tart","value":null},
{"id":"ApricotEvespudding","key":"Apricot Eve's pudding","value":null},
{"id":"Apricotfreezerjam","key":"Apricot freezer jam","value":null}
]}
```

Querying on Complex Data

Because you define the parameters and content of the view, you can use this to produce and support different methods of accessing and sharing the information. For example, what if you wanted to support accessing recipe information by using the ingredients from the recipe?

The emit() function we used in the original view can be called multiple times within your map function, each time outputting a row. Because each generated row contains the attached value and the document ID that generated the row, we can use this to query the recipe data by the ingredient, and get the recipe information in return.

The view definition below shows a new view that emits a row of data based on the ingredient text by iterating over the ingredient list from each recipe document, and emitting each ingredient name.

```
function(doc) {
    if (doc.ingredients) {
        for(i=0;i<doc.ingredients.length;i++) {
            emit(doc.ingredients[i].ingredient, null);
        }
    }
}
```

Querying this using the same query values as last time, but using the view by_ingredient, we get the following list of recipes:

```
{
    "total_rows" : 26468,
    "rows" : [
        {
            "value" : null,
            "id" : "Jamaicandelightcocktail",
            "key" : "apricot brandy"
        },
        {
            "value" : null,
            "id" : "Appleandcinnamonpuffs",
            "key" : "apricot jam"
        },
```

```
{
    "value" : null,
    "id" : "Apricotcoconuttart",
    "key" : "apricot jam"
},
{
    "value" : null,
    "id" : "Coffeeandgrapecheesecake",
    "key" : "apricot jam"
},
{
    "value" : null,
    "id" : "Continentalmueslitorte",
    "key" : "apricot jam"
},
{
    "value" : null,
    "id" : "Frenchappleflan",
    "key" : "apricot jam"
},
{
    "value" : null,
    "id" : "Fruitybakedparcels",
    "key" : "apricot jam"
},
{
    "value" : null,
    "id" : "LastminuteChristmascake",
    "key" : "apricot jam"
},
{
    "value" : null,
    "id" : "Normandybreadandbutterpudding",
    "key" : "apricot jam"
},
{
    "value" : null,
    "id" : "Sachertorte",
    "key" : "apricot jam"
},
{
    "value" : null,
    "id" : "Sultanacitrustruffles",
    "key" : "apricot jam"
},
{
    "value" : null,
    "id" : "Trufflecake",
    "key" : "apricot jam"
},
{
    "value" : null,
    "id" : "Welshgingercake",
    "key" : "apricot jam"
},
```

```
    {
        "value" : null,
        "id" : "Tropicaljuicecocktail",
        "key" : "apricot juice"
    }
    ],
    "offset" : 1371
}
```

Now we have all the recipes that contain some kind of apricot ingredient.

For a view like this, the chances are we are really looking for a specific single value, such as Lemon Sole. In this case, we can use the key argument to the query:

```
http://127.0.0.1:5984/recipes/_design/simple/_view/by_ingredient?key=%22lemon%20sole
%22
```

Which in turn outputs the recipes that contain Lemon Sole:

```
{
    "total_rows" : 26468,
    "rows" : [
        {
            "value" : null,
            "id" : "Lemonsoleenpapillote",
            "key" : "lemon sole"
        },
        {
            "value" : null,
            "id" : "Soleandsalmonfling",
            "key" : "lemon sole"
        },
        {
            "value" : null,
            "id" : "Soleandsalmonroulade",
            "key" : "lemon sole"
        },
        {
            "value" : null,
            "id" : "Soleduxelles",
            "key" : "lemon sole"
        }
    ],
    "offset" : 14323
}
```

Querying Compound Data

So far we've looked at single data points (Lemon Sole) and ranges (Apricots). But if you wanted to search by more complex means, such as all the recipes with Trout that take less than 10 minutes, then you need to construct a different view.

Although this sounds complicated, the reality is that for the vast majority of database queries, the actual query structure is the same, only the values differ. Once you have created your database, and then your views, you will eventually have developed the suite of views necessary to support the different query and list information that you need.

CouchDB supports this by allowing you to output a compound type as the key generated by the `emit()` call. In this case, let's output an array containing the ingredient and the recipe cooking time:

```
function(doc) {
    if (doc.ingredients) {
        for(i=0;i<doc.ingredients.length;i++) {
            if (doc.ingredients[i].ingredient !== null)
                emit([doc.ingredients[i].ingredient, parseInt(doc.cooktime)], null);
        }
    }
}
```

This will output an array that contains the ingredient text and the cooking time. To query it, we need to provide a JSON value to the key parameters. So to perform our original query we might use:

http://127.0.0.1:5984/recipes/_design/recipe/_view/by_ingredient_time?startkey=%5B%22trout%22,0%5D&endkey=%5B%22trout%22,150%5D

This generates a list of all the recipes using trout that can be cooked in fewer than 10 minutes:

```
{
    "total_rows" : 25215,
    "rows" : [
        {
            "value" : null,
            "id" : "Searedtroutbruschettawithhorseradish",
            "key" : [
                "trout",
                3
            ]
        },
        {
            "value" : null,
            "id" : "Barbecuedtroutwithfennelbutter",
            "key" : [
                "trout",
                6
            ]
        },
    ...
    ],
    "offset" : 23299
}
```

Reduce Functions

Often the information that you are searching or reporting on needs to be summarized or reduced. There are a number of different occasions when this can be useful, for example, if you want to obtain a count of all the items of a particular type, such as comments, recipes matching an ingredient, or blog entries against a keyword.

Alternatively, views can be used for performing sums, such as totaling all of the invoice values for a single client, or totaling up the preparation and cooking times in a recipe.

In each of the above cases, the raw data is the information from one or more rows of information produced by a call to emit(). The input data, each record generated by the emit() call, is reduced and grouped together to produce a new record in the output.

A good example of reduction functions in action with our recipe example is the sort of display typical when browsing recipes. Here you might want to show recipes by their keyword, then provide a count of the number of recipes by the keyword. The view uses the built-in _count function:

```
"by_keyword": {
    "map": "function(doc) { if (doc.keywords) { for(i=0;i<doc.keywords.length;i++)
{ emit(doc.keywords[i], null); } } }",
    "reduce": "_count"
},
```

When querying, we have to specify the group level (the default is 0, which would provide a count of all the rows generated by emit()). The query looks like this:

```
http://localhost:5984/recipes/_design/simple/_view/by_keyword?group_level=1
```

 The reduce function within a view is optional, but if defined, the reduce function is automatically applied to the view output. You can switch this off by adding the reduce=false option to the query.

The resulting view result looks like this:

```
{"rows":[
{"key":"convenience@add bread for complete meal","value":234},
{"key":"convenience@add jacket potato for a complete meal","value":110},
{"key":"convenience@add pasta for a complete meal","value":44},
{"key":"convenience@add rice for a complete meal","value":133},
{"key":"convenience@serve with salad for complete meal","value":214},
{"key":"cook method.hob, oven, grill@grill","value":135},
{"key":"cook method.hob, oven, grill@grill / oven","value":8},
{"key":"cook method.hob, oven, grill@hob","value":1036},
{"key":"cook method.hob, oven, grill@hob / grill","value":98},
{"key":"cook method.hob, oven, grill@hob / grill / oven","value":8},
{"key":"cook method.hob, oven, grill@hob / oven","value":469},
{"key":"cook method.hob, oven, grill@oven","value":361},
...
```

The output is trimmed here, but you can see the recipe information has been grouped together by the keyword text, with the value showing a count of the recipes that include that keyword.

Let's take a closer look at the internal workings, but simplify our data set slightly so that the process and calculations are easier. We'll use this sample data:

```
{
    "city" : "Paris",
    "sales" : 13000,
    "name" : "James",
},
{
    "city" : "Tokyo",
    "sales" : 20000,
    "name" : "James",
},
{
    "city" : "Paris",
    "sales" : 5000,
    "name" : "James",
},
{
    "city" : "Paris",
    "sales" : 22000,
    "name" : "John",
},
{
    "city" : "London",
    "sales" : 3000,
    "name" : "John",
},
{
    "city" : "London",
    "sales" : 7000,
    "name" : "John",
},
{
    "city" : "London",
    "sales" : 7000,
    "name" : "Adam",
},
{
    "city" : "Paris",
    "sales" : 19000,
    "name" : "Adam",
},
{
    "city" : "Tokyo",
    "sales" : 17000,
    "name" : "Adam",
}
```

When using a reduce function the reduction is applied as follows:

- For each record of input, the corresponding reduce function is applied on the row generated from the emit() call in the map function. For example, using the following design document:

```
{
    "language": "javascript",
    "views": {
        "bynamecity": {
            "map": "function(doc) { emit([doc.name,doc.city],doc.sales)}",
            "reduce": "_sum"
        }
    }
}
```

The key is output using an array of both the name and the city for the sales. The reduce function uses the built-in _sum function. Outputting the view without the reduce function produces the following information:

```
{
    "total_rows" : 9,
    "rows" : [
        {
            "value" : 7000,
            "id" : "64f4057ad37fdd9bc2ccd808ca01c717",
            "key" : [
                "Adam",
                "London"
            ]
        },
        {
            "value" : 19000,
            "id" : "64f4057ad37fdd9bc2ccd808ca01d629",
            "key" : [
                "Adam",
                "Paris"
            ]
        },
        ...
    ],
    "offset" : 0
}
```

Calling the view with reduction enabled, we receive a sum of all the records from the view:

```
{
    "rows" : [
        {
            "value" : 113000,
            "key" : null
        }
    ]
}
```

- Results are grouped on the key from the call to emit(). As shown in the previous example, the reduction operates by taking the key as the group value and using this as the basis of the reduction.

- By using an array as the key, you can group to multiple levels. There are times you may want to perform a reduction on a compound value. For example, on both the name of the salesman and the city in which they did their business. You can achieve this by using an array as your key and specifying the `group_level` parameter. Group level 1 uses the first element of the key array as the group value:

```
{
    "rows" : [
        {
            "value" : 43000,
            "key" : [
                "Adam"
            ]
        },
        {
            "value" : 38000,
            "key" : [
                "James"
            ]
        },
        {
            "value" : 32000,
            "key" : [
                "John"
            ]
        }
    ]
}
```

Group level 2 uses the first *and* second elements of the key array as the group value:

```
{
    "rows" : [
        {
          "value" : 18000,
          "id" : "James",
          "key" : ["James", "Paris"]
        },
        {
          "value" : 20000,
          "id" : "James",
          "key" : ["James", "Tokyo"],
        },
    ...
    ]
}
```

In this case, because the group level of 2 was specified, the first two elements of the array provided in the key have been used as the collation key.

You can also output null values within your `map` function, which can be used in combination with your `reduce` function to provide summary and grouping information to combine different information types into the output.

Whenever the reduce function is called, the generated view content contains the same key and value fields for each row, but the key is the selected group (or an array of the group elements according to the group level) and the value is the computed reduction value.

CouchDB includes three built-in reduce functions: _count, _sum, and _stats.

Reduce functions have one final trick up their sleeves: the results of the reduction are stored in the index along with the rest of the view information. This means that when accessing the result of a reduce function in your view is only accessing the index content, and therefore is very low impact compared to calculating the values live when the view is accessed.

Built-in _count

The _count function provides a simple count of the input rows from the map function, using the keys and group level to provide to provide a count of the correlated items. The values generated during the map() stage are ignored.

Enabling the reduce() function and using a group level of 1 would produce:

```
{
    "rows" : [
        {
          "value" : 3,
          "key" : [
            "Adam"
          ]
        },
        {
          "value" : 3,
          "key" : [
            "James"
          ]
        },
        {
          "value" : 3,
          "key" : [
            "John"
          ]
        }
    ]
}
```

The reduction has produced a new result set with the key as an array based on the first element of the array from the map output. The value is the count of the number of records collated by the first element.

Using a group level of 2 would generate the following:

```
{
    "rows" : [
        {
          "value" : 1,
```

```
          "key" : [
             "Adam",
             "London"
          ]
     },
     {
       "value" : 1,
       "key" : [
          "Adam",
          "Paris"
       ]
     },
     {
       "value" : 1,
       "key" : [
          "Adam",
          "Tokyo"
       ]
     },
     {
       "value" : 2,
       "key" : [
          "James",
          "Paris"
       ]
     },
     {
       "value" : 1,
       "key" : [
          "James",
          "Tokyo"
       ]
     },
     {
       "value" : 2,
       "key" : [
          "John",
          "London"
       ]
     },
     {
       "value" : 1,
       "key" : [
          "John",
          "Paris"
       ]
     }
   ]
}
```

Now the counts are for the keys matching both the first two elements of the map output.

Built-in _sum

The built-in _sum functions collates the output from the map function call, this time summing up the information in the value for each row. The information can either be a single number or an array of numbers.

 The input values must be a number, not a string-representation of a number. The entire Map/Reduce will fail if the reduce input is not in the correct format. You should use the parseInt() or parseFloat() function calls within your map() function stage to ensure that the input data is a number.

For example, using the same sales source data, accessing the group level 1 view would produce the total sales for each salesman:

```
{
  "rows" : [
    {
      "value" : 43000,
      "key" : [
        "Adam"
      ]
    },
    {
      "value" : 38000,
      "key" : [
        "James"
      ]
    },
    {
      "value" : 32000,
      "key" : [
        "John"
      ]
    }
  ]
}
```

Using a group level of 2, you get the information summarized by salesman and city:

```
{
  "rows" : [
    {
      "value" : 7000,
      "key" : [
        "Adam",
        "London"
      ]
    },
    {
      "value" : 19000,
      "key" : [
        "Adam",
```

```
              "Paris"
            ]
          },
          {
            "value" : 17000,
            "key" : [
                "Adam",
                "Tokyo"
            ]
          },
          {
            "value" : 18000,
            "key" : [
                "James",
                "Paris"
            ]
          },
          {
            "value" : 20000,
            "key" : [
                "James",
                "Tokyo"
            ]
          },
          {
            "value" : 10000,
            "key" : [
                "John",
                "London"
            ]
          },
          {
            "value" : 22000,
            "key" : [
                "John",
                "Paris"
            ]
          }
      ]
  }
```

Built-in _stats

The _stats built-in produces statistical calculations for the input data. Like the _sum
call, the source information should be a number. The generated statistics include the
sum, count, minimum (min), maximum (max), and sum squared (sumsqr) of the input
rows.

Using the sales data, a slightly truncated output would be:

```
{
    "rows" : [
        {
          "value" : {
              "count" : 3,
```

```
        "min" : 7000,
        "sumsqr" : 699000000,
        "max" : 19000,
        "sum" : 43000
      },
      "key" : [
        "Adam"
      ]
    },
    {
      "value" : {
        "count" : 3,
        "min" : 5000,
        "sumsqr" : 594000000,
        "max" : 20000,
        "sum" : 38000
      },
      "key" : [
        "James"
      ]
    },
    {
      "value" : {
        "count" : 3,
        "min" : 3000,
        "sumsqr" : 542000000,
        "max" : 22000,
        "sum" : 32000
      },
      "key" : [
        "John"
      ]
    }
  ]
}
```

The same fields in the output value are provided for each of the reduced output rows.

Custom reduce functions

You can write your own reduce functions to produce custom reduction operations on your data. Custom reduce functions are easy to write, but you have to know a few of the rules for doing so. Probably the most important aspect to remember is that a reduce function may be called by itself to complete the reduction functionality. This process is called rereduce. The reduce function definition identifies this by using a third argument to the call to the reduce function:

```
function (key, values, rereduce) {
    return sum(values);
}
```

The function should return the values that you want to be returned by the reduction process.

The rereduce is a boolean value that is used to indicate when the reduce function is being called by itself (i.e., in rereduce mode). For a standard reduction (no rereduce, where rereduce is false), the arguments are:

- Key will be an array, the elements of which are an array consisting of the key and document ID generated by the `emit()` calls within your map function
- Values is an array of the values generated from the value argument of your `emit()` function call. This is an array of the values from the documents referenced in the keys elements.

For example, when performing the reduce on the sample sales data a reduction function might be provided with:

```
reduce([ [ "James", "James"], [ "Adam", "Adam" ], [ "John", "John" ] ],[ 13000, 5000, 10000 ], false);
```

Notice in the above that we have been provided the keys of three items, and the values of each corresponding item. Effectively this is equivalent to:

```
reduce([ [key1,id1], [key2,id2], [key3,id3] ], [value1,value2,value3], false)
```

If the function is being called in rereduce mode, then the rereduce value will be true, the keys will be null, and the values will be one or more values returned from the previous calls to the reduce function. For example:

```
reduce(null, [28000, 40000, 10000], true)
```

To put this into perspective, we can reproduce the _sum built-in function like this:

```
function(keys,values,rereduce)
{
    var sum = 0;
    for(var idx in values) {
        sum = sum + values[idx];
    }
    return sum;
}
```

Here we just take each of the values in the array of values supplied, sum them together, and return them. In this case, the output information for a rereduce is irrelevant because the values will be in the same format. We return a simple value, which will be supplied as part of an array of values in the event of a rereduce.

However, it is possible to return compound values. For example, say you wanted to produce a view that provided both the count of the items, and the sum of the value. In this case, the reduce would process the raw values (sales), but the output would be the count and the sum of the values supplied. The function in this case would look like the following:

```
function(keys,values,rereduce) {
    var count = 0;
    var sum = 0;
```

```
if (rereduce) {
    for(var idx in values) {
        count = count + values[idx][0];
        sum = sum + values[idx][1];
    }
}
else {
    for(var idx in values) {
        count = count + 1;
        sum = sum + values[idx];
    }
}
return [count,sum];
}
```

When the function is called merely as a reduce function, we can just count the entries and add up the values, but we return an array of the count and sum. In rereduce mode, we need to extract the values from the array returned by the reduce stage, hence the two different formats.

Error handling in views

CouchDB has been designed to be fairly resilient to problems that you create within the views. In most cases, CouchDB will try to create the view definition even if there are occasional issues in the content and output format. For example, if you create a view that outputs a field where the field is not defined in a document, instead of completely failing to generate your view, CouchDB will output a null value for each document.

Mostly this is a huge help, because it ensures that minor errors don't completely defeat the benefits of defining your view. The downside is that it can sometimes be difficult to determine a problem if you find your view isn't generating the information you expect.

Errors generated by CouchDB are recorded in the CouchDB log, which you can access from within CouchDB using *http://127.0.0.1:5984/_log*.

If you want to monitor specific values within your views, unfortunately, you cannot directly debug the progress and output, but you can call the log() function to output information in your views. This generates entries in your log file prefixed by the Log tag:

```
[Mon, 31 Oct 2011 13:31:34 GMT] [info] [<0.31248.20>] OS Process #Port<0.7491> Log ::
Root vegetables baked in cream with garlic

[Mon, 31 Oct 2011 13:31:34 GMT] [info] [<0.31248.20>] OS Process #Port<0.7491> Log ::
Carrot and thyme roulade with onion and garlic cream

[Mon, 31 Oct 2011 13:31:34 GMT] [info] [<0.31248.20>] OS Process #Port<0.7491> Log ::
Bacon and pesto pasta salad

[Mon, 31 Oct 2011 13:31:34 GMT] [info] [<0.31248.20>] OS Process #Port<0.7491> Log ::
Pork balls with tomato sauce and spaghetti
```

Temporary views

Before we move on, there is one final convenience facility for CouchDB views. Defining and uploading views for the purposes of testing can be a little time consuming and complex. To simplify the process, you can create a temporary view.

To use a temporary view, you submit the view information as the HTTP body in a request to the _temp_view component for your database. For example, we can rewrite the recipe by title view as a temporary view using curl like this:

```
curl -X POST -H 'Content-type: application/json' \
    http://127.0.0.1:5984/recipes/_temp_view \
    -d '{"map": "function(doc) {emit(doc.title,null)}"}'
```

Temporary views like this are only good for testing your view definition. The information is not sorted in any way (eliminating many of the benefits of the view) and because this process immediately executes the view on your data, the process is processor intensive.

Querying View Results

When querying the view results, you can use the query arguments shown in the table below to limit and manipulate your query. Some of the key query parameters are:

descending
> By default, CouchDB sorts the keys and outputs the view in ascending order (i.e., A-Z). By specifying descending=true, the view results will be output in descending order (i.e., Z-A).
>
> One artifact of this process is that if you are searching for a range of items then you must also reverse the startkey and endkey values, because the order in which CouchDB will reach has changed. For example, the query:
>
> ```
> /recipes/_design/simple/_view/bytitle?startkey=Lasagne&endkey=Pasta
> ```
>
> Should be written as:
>
> ```
> /recipes/_design/simple/_view/bytitle?
> descending=true&endkey=Lasagne&startkey=Pasta
> ```

limit
> Limit the output the specified number of rows. For example, to limit the output to 10 rows:
>
> ```
> /recipes/_design/simple/_view/bytitle?limit=10
> ```

skip
> Skip the specified number of rows before starting the output. For example:
>
> ```
> /recipes/_design/simple/_view/bytitle?skip=100
> ```

CouchDB will process 100 rows of view output, and then only start outputting row values on the 101st row.

You can use this in combination with the `limit` parameter to paginate through the output, but this is a relatively expensive operation, as CouchDB still actually accesses the row information.

stale

Allow stale views. Because CouchDB only rebuilds the view index; when the view is accessed, it can mean that there is a delay between requesting the view information and the output being generated, because the view index must be updated. If you are not worried about updating the view index (or including any records) since the last time the view was updated, you can use `stale=true` to use the existing view index and not update the view data. This is quicker, but may output stale information as it won't include any of the recent document updates, deletions, and inserts since the view was last updated.

There are some other possible values and query arguments. Check The CouchDB API (*http://docs.couchbase.org/couchbase-api/couchbase-api-design.html#couchbase-api-design_db-design-designdoc-view-viewname_get*) for more information.

Lists

Lists are to views what shows are to individual documents. In a very simple way they perform exactly the same function. They output the results from each row generated by a view, and transform it into any format you want. As with a show, you can use this to output as HTML, XML, formatted JSON, even CSV if that is what you need.

Unlike a show, a list has to deal with the slightly more complex information in the form of one or more rows of generated information, rather than just a single document.

The basics of the list function are similar to the view and show functions we have already seen. You can specify more than one list function in a design document. However, you must specify the list and the view that you are using to output information within the same design document.

The function definition for a list is as follows:

```
function(head, req) {}
```

The `head` argument contains core information about the view being supplied to the list function, specifically it's the information beyond the row data (i.e., the total number of rows and the number of skipped, or offset, rows):

```
{
    total_rows:2667,
    offset:0
}
```

The `req` is a much more complex structure and contains all of the information about the request, including any HTTP headers, stored cookie information for the domain, security data, the request path, a UUID, client and server information, and even database information for the database being accessed. This is beyond the scope of this book, but for reference, the structure looks like this:

```
{
    "info" : {
        "compact_running" : false,
        "doc_count" : 2671,
        "db_name" : "recipes",
        "purge_seq" : 0,
        "committed_update_seq" : 2719,
        "doc_del_count" : 1,
        "disk_format_version" : 5,
        "update_seq" : 2719,
        "instance_start_time" : "1319627005264155",
        "disk_size" : 17121380
    },
    "headers" : {
        "Connection" : "keep-alive",
        "User-Agent" : "Mozilla/5.0 (Macintosh; Intel Mac OS X 10_7_2) AppleWebKit/
534.51.22 (KHTML, like Gecko) Version/5.1.1 Safari/534.51.22",
        "Cache-Control" : "max-age=0",
        "Accept-Encoding" : "gzip, deflate",
        "Accept" : "text/html,application/xhtml+xml,application/xml;q=0.9,*/*;q=0.8",
        "Accept-Language" : "en-us",
        "Host" : "localhost:5984"
    },
    "userCtx" : {
        "roles" : [
            "_admin"
        ],
        "db" : "recipes",
        "name" : null
    },
    "query" : {
        "limit" : "10"
    },
    "cookie" : {},
    "form" : {},
    "path" : [
        "recipes",
        "_design",
        "simple",
        "_list",
        "by_title",
        "by_title"
    ],
    "uuid" : "64f4057ad37fdd9bc2ccd808ca01fbae",
    "body" : "undefined",
    "peer" : "127.0.0.1",
    "id" : null,
    "method" : "GET"
}
```

Both the head and request information allow you to view and parse the request much more closely. For example, you can extract the query elements from the requested URL or a form to generate and output different information.

The core definition of the remainder of the list function is surprisingly straightforward. The function itself is called only once for the entire group of documents supplied to it. So, unlike a show, we have to manually iterate over the content.

To do that, we use the getRow() function in a while statement to get each row of the generated view. For example, to create a bulleted list of the recipes, with a link to the show that will display them:

```
function (head,req) {

    start({ "headers": {
        "Content-type" : "text/html"
            }
    });

    send('<ul>');

    var row;

    while (row = getRow()) {
        send('<li><a href="/recipes/_design/detail/_show/recipe/'
            + row.id + '\">' + row.key + '</a></li>');
    }

    send('</ul>');
}
```

In the above example, everything before the while is sent before the individual rows of the view are processed. The start() function is used to output the HTTP headers, in this case, an HTML content type so that we can generate an HTML list. Then we output the opening HTML bullet list tag.

The while block gets each row of the generated view and puts it into the variable row. Remember that the output of a view is a row of information in the form of the document ID, key, and value of the generated information. Once the view data has been processed, we close the HTML list.

The complete definition as part of a design document is shown below:

```
{
    "language": "javascript",
    "views": {
        "by_title": {
            "map": "function(doc) { if (doc.title != null) emit(doc.title, null) }"
        }
    },
    "lists": {
        "by_title": "function (head,req) { start({'headers': { 'Content-type': 'text/
html' }}); send('<html><ul>'); var row; while(row = getRow()) { send('<li><a href=\"/
recipes/_design/detail/_show/recipe/' + row.id + '\">' + row.key + '</a></li>'); }
```

```
send('</ul></html>'); }"
    },
    "shows": {
    "simple": "function(doc, req) { var output; output = '<h1>' + doc.title + '</h1>';
output += '<p>' + doc.subtitle + '</p>'; output += '<h2>Ingredients</h2><ul>';
for(i=0;i<doc.ingredients.length;i++) { output += '<li>' + doc.ingredients[i].measure
+ ' ' + doc.ingredients[i].\
ingredient + '</li>';} output += '</ul><h2>Method</h2><ol>';
for(i=0;i<doc.method.length;i++) { output += '<li>' + doc.method[i].text } output +=
'</ol>'; return output; }"
    }
}
```

To access a list you use a URL of the format:

```
/DBNAME/_design/DESIGNDOC/_list/LISTNAME/VIEWNAME
```

In the above example we could access the view for the design document simple:

```
http://localhost:5984/recipes/_design/simple/_list/by_title/by_title
```

The above design document becomes a completely self-contained solution for querying, listing, and viewing recipes from the database. The view outputs the recipe by their title. The list formats the recipes as a nice HTML list, with each recipe as a link to the corresponding show function to display the recipe content.

About the Author

Martin "MC" Brown, a professional writer for over 15 years, is the author and contributor to over 26 books covering an array of topics, including programming, system management, and web technologies. His expertise spans myriad development languages and platforms—Perl, Python, Java, JavaScript, Basic, Pascal, Modula-2, C, C++, Rebol, Gawk, Shellscript, Windows, Solaris, Linux, BeOS, Microsoft WP, Mac OS and more. The combination has resulted in expertise in web programming, systems management and integration, and XML and DocBook technologies for writing and publishing documentation. He is also a former LAMP Technologies Editor for Linux-World magazine and a regular contributor to ServerWatch.com, LinuxPlanet, ComputerWorld, and IBM developerWorks. As a Subject Matter Expert for Microsoft, he provided technical input to their Windows Server and certification teams. He draws on a rich and varied background as founding member of a leading UK ISP, systems manager and IT consultant for an advertising agency and Internet solutions group, technical specialist for an intercontinental ISP network, and database designer and programmer—and as a self-confessed compulsive consumer of computing hardware and software. In his pre-writing life, he spent more than 10 years designing and managing mixed platform environments. As a result he has developed a rare talent of being able to convey the benefits and intricacies of his subject with equal measures of enthusiasm, professionalism, in-depth knowledge, and insight. Formerly as a technical writer, he spent time building both the documentation system and writing content for MySQL and the MySQL groups within Sun and then Oracle. MC is currently the VP of Documentation for Couchbase and is responsible for all published documentation, training programme and content, and the Couchbase Community.

Get even more for your money.

Join the O'Reilly Community, and register the O'Reilly books you own. It's free, and you'll get:

- $4.99 ebook upgrade offer
- 40% upgrade offer on O'Reilly print books
- Membership discounts on books and events
- Free lifetime updates to ebooks and videos
- Multiple ebook formats, DRM FREE
- Participation in the O'Reilly community
- Newsletters
- Account management
- 100% Satisfaction Guarantee

Signing up is easy:

1. **Go to: oreilly.com/go/register**
2. **Create an O'Reilly login.**
3. **Provide your address.**
4. **Register your books.**

Note: English-language books only

To order books online:
oreilly.com/store

For questions about products or an order:
orders@oreilly.com

To sign up to get topic-specific email announcements and/or news about upcoming books, conferences, special offers, and new technologies:
elists@oreilly.com

For technical questions about book content:
booktech@oreilly.com

To submit new book proposals to our editors:
proposals@oreilly.com

O'Reilly books are available in multiple DRM-free ebook formats. For more information:
oreilly.com/ebooks

O'REILLY®

Spreading the knowledge of innovators   oreilly.com

Have it your way.